ACKNOWLEDGMENT -

"Let the truth be known...all that I have accomplished and all that I have done has been based on Carole...who has been and still is ..."the wind beneath my wings". Thank you sweet joy of my life for all that you have done for our children, our grandchildren, our pets and your adoring husband! None of us could have done anything without you!"

~Henry J. Mankin, 2007

1

CHAPTER 1: INTRODUCTION – by Keith Mankin

The world is full of surgeons. From the very day that humans discovered how to hone a cutting edge, some member of the community became expert in using the tool to remove unwanted excrescences. Invasive treatments continued to develop as a trade until deep in the seventeenth century when the Enlightenment encouraged learned souls to not only question and explore the body but also try to improve it in the face of disease.

The treatment of bone disorders was primitive for a longer period of time. Any member of society with large hands and strong arms could set a broken bone and lash on a splint. Deformities of limb and spine, or any condition other than acute injuries tended to be neglected as the work of God or fate. With the advent of radiographic imaging, doctors began to understand the skeleton in life. Rather than the bleached bones of the anatomy lab, they found a living and changing organ. Again the appreciation of anatomy and pathology led to the desire to cure, but it was just over a hundred years ago that the first dedicated bone doctors emerged. They termed their field orthopaedics, Greek for 'straight child' and thus differentiated themselves from the bone-setters of yore.

Even as the field became ever more sophisticated with the study of tumors, infections and crippling diseases such as poliomyelitis, a dichotomy emerged which is still in force today. The vast majority of practitioners are surgeons who ply their field with care and skill but without the curiosity or the time to research or innovate the field. In every generation there is a smaller group of specialists who can see beyond the still limited scope of knowledge. They will look at a given problem not through the spectrum of what is already known but with

3

the vision to access new and novel areas of inquiry. A very small handful can do this while also treating scores of patients and teaching generations of disciples.

Henry Mankin is one of these privileged few.

In a clinical career spanning more than fifty years and a teaching life that has added almost two decades to that, he has envisioned, innovated, instructed and cared enough to fill discrete careers as a surgeon, a researcher, a teacher and mentor. If his life included only these accomplishments then it would be remarkable indeed.

But he has also embodied aspects of a great American success story as well. He is a first generation native born to parents who fled persecution and grappled with assimilation into a new and changing society. His childhood encompassed the Great Depression and the Second World War. His rapid ascendency in his field jarred the staid fixtures of orthopaedics and other long-established medical institutions. His global reputation as a teacher, surgeon and researcher shattered a culture of international insularity. And his accomplishments overwhelmed the long-standing condescension of the entire medical world towards the specialty of orthopaedics.

His is a great story to be told. And since he is a marvelous story teller whose many attributes do not include humility, it is a story that he is delighted to share. What follows are Henry Mankin's memoirs, clarified and extended, with due deference, by one of his (natural) sons and disciples (naturally).

My dad is obsessed with immortality. Not truly living forever (Who would want that, he asks?). But rather in always being relevant, always being a hero to the succeeding groups of men and women who work in medicine and safeguard the musculoskeletal system.

4

"In the Jewish faith," he says, "we have no heaven, no eternal afterlife. Our immortality comes in the prolonged memories of our children, our grandchildren. That's why we light a candle on the anniversary of our loved ones' deaths.

"In medicine, immortality comes from the people you have taught. Your students are your children and carry your memory to new generations."

Every so often, giving a lecture at a meeting or a hospital where I have never been and which has never hosted my father (they are rare), I will hear an attending physician provide a helpful fact to the students – in medicine we call them 'pearls' – and I will recognize it as one of my dad's. The lineage can be traced back – the provider learned it from his mentor who learned it from her mentor who did a fellowship with someone who trained with my father. At those times, I see my dad's legacy is secure, his immortality persists.

I have often been asked if Henry has been a role model to me. On reflection, I have to answer, no. His footsteps are far too large and deep for me to clamber about in without getting hurt. But he is and always will be a source of wonder and inspiration.

CHAPTER 2: MEMORIES AND PRE-MEMORIES OF CROMBIE STREET

[For the vast majority of people living in Russia, the turn of the twentieth century brought no appreciable difference to their lives. The vast, unnamed and disenfranchised rural population had no change in lifestyle or standard of living for several centuries. The Russian peasant, toiling in agrarian serfdom, may have been vaguely aware of progress such as plumbing or electricity, but few would have seen these wonders and none could have expected to ever benefit for them. Progress was meant for the ruling class, the landed elite who still held sway in this stubbornly feudal society.

The underclass of Russian Jews found life even worse around the century's turn. A Russian born peasant could not own land but at least had some security for home and family. He could not vote, but could at least rely on feudal protection from his landlord in times of crisis. But a Jewish family had no rights and no security. They might settle and form a village, a closed society secluded by their institutional and religious otherness. They might live for years in comparative peace, but at the whim of the powerful or even of the peasants themselves they could be displaced with violent demonstrations called pogroms, driven from land and home without the protection of any local laws.

In the fragile and desperate turn of the century the pogroms were escalating. The Jews were a convenient scapegoat. The uneducated rural populations could be assuaged by action against what was perceived as a common enemy or their mutinous urges satisfied by a public show of violence against a group of people even less privileged than they. Even though most of the Jews in this region had been born and raised in the Russian empire, they were never accepted as natives. They were easily displaced.

Unlike a later generation in Central and Eastern Europe when the displacement took more lethal forms, the Russian Jews were harassed and scarred but left with the gift of life. For the luckiest, there was even opportunity of escape. Channels opened to the west first Europe and then in the United States. In New York City and other cities along the east coast, the influx of Jewish people formed tight communities, shockingly crowded for hitherto rural people. Many kept moving west into the Ohio River Valley and other parts of the central plains, where newer such as Pittsburgh, PA, in need of population and without many of the long-standing prejudices of the East Coast or the South, waited with somewhat open arms and the possibility of easier assimilation.

It was to this community that Henry's parents, Hyman Mankin and Mary Simons arrived with their families in the earliest years of the newborn century. -

It has been a long time since I left Crombie Street and a detailed recollection of the way things were is not as easy as I once thought it would be. I was born there (more accurately at the Magee Hospital in the Oakland district of Pittsburgh, Pennslvania) and lived at 6307 Crombie Street in Squirrel Hill from 1928 until my third year of medical school in 1952. Things come back to me at times (sometimes stimulated by a scene, a sound or even an odor) and some of it is like yesterday...others like the names of people who were a part of those early days have faded like they have. Anyway, I shall try to look back at some of those memories and for the sake of our children, grandchildren and all that follow recall as best I can Mary, Hymie, Milton, Arthur and the days on Crombie Street.

The House and the Neighborhood:

The house at 6307 Crombie Street was one away from the corner of Crombie and Tilbury Street. Tilbury and Beechwood Boulevard are parallel streets running east, I believe and Crombie Street was a short, narrow but rather steep passage between the two....it was only one block long. The incline was so steep that early on the street was in cobble stones; and driving on it was considered to be hazardous in winter.   Conversely, sledding was wonderful for the kids. It was not much of a thoroughfare...most of the people who walked or drove on it had some business there.

The house itself was small by any standards...but I presume was considered luxurious by my parents and brothers when they moved from their early home on Bluff Street (I never saw that house...and don't even know where it is or was). The building was two stories in height with a porch...the entry door was on the right side of the porch. One entered into a tiny entry hall and slightly to the right against the outside wall was a flight

8

of stairs to the second floor. The hall itself led by way of a narrow passageway to a breakfast alcove and from there into a kitchen; or if one turned left through an archway, into a medium sized living room and dining room which occupied the front and back central parts of the house. Early in our life on Crombie Street Mary decided that she needed more room for her family and arranged for the back porch, initially off the kitchen to be extended and closed in so as to provide a new kitchen at the back of the house, a closed in porch in the back (behind the dining room)...and thus convert the old kitchen into a breakfast room. It was a big undertaking for depression days, but clearly we needed the room and explains why in a square house the kitchen is extends further back than the dining room.

Upstairs were three bedrooms and a bath...the master bedroom in the back for Mary and Hymie and a small front bedroom for Milton and a bigger one for Arthur and me. The basement was originally just that. It had a lot of storage space for trunks and boxes, a toilet where Hymie did the crossword puzzle every morning, a pair of large gray sinks for the wash and a furnace which originally burned coal and subsequently was converted to gas. Mary did all of that...she put coal in the furnace (from a pile outside the cellar door), did the laundry by hand, hung things out to dry in the back yard, and kept it all spotless. We acquired first a wringer and then a washing machine in the mid-thirties and I think that was a big help to Mary on her Mondays. The rest of the space was originally just storage but slowly it was converted to a study ....mostly by Arthur and Mary so that we (Arthur and later I) could have a place to work at school work, our stamp collection, etc. It seems to me that Arthur built a crystal radio set there and one of my first reminiscences of the basement was listening to it using earphones. There was a work bench, some shelving, bookcases and a second hand desk which was lit by some fluorescent lighting fixtures that Arthur put in. There was even a bootleg telephone. I liked that desk and enjoyed working there during high school. It was quiet and I could work without interruption.

The two major features of that house as far as Mary was concerned were the gardens (a large one in the back and another smaller and more decorative one in the front) and the porch in the front. She loved both gardens and had the proverbial green thumb. She grew flowers in both until the war and then turned the larger one in the back into a Victory Garden...with onions, tomatoes and some of the largest cucumbers that ever grew. As to the porch, it was overlooking the front garden and was really very elegant. The front garden was full of roses (despite Arthur's alleged rose fever) and lots of other flowers such as lilacs and honeysuckle. I particularly loved the morning glories. At one end of the porch we had a swing and some wicker chairs with soft comfortable seats and backs. At one point (I am not sure when) we bought a glider and a porch rug. To close it off, we had striped awnings on the sides and ivy which grew on a wooden trellis over the front so that the porch was "private" and screened off from the street. There was no air-conditioning in those days so the porch became the place where we lived in the summer time. It wasn't just day times, but evening as well and we would all sit and talk and watch the world go by (or at least the Crombie Street world) until it cooled off enough to go to sleep. I remember many summer nights sitting there in my pajamas listening to conversations in Yiddish or English (and sometimes in Lithuanian when they didn't want me to understand) and falling asleep and having to be carried up to bed! I have always wanted a porch like that in my own home...it was really very special but I never had one (at least so far!).

I suppose one of the reasons that Mary and Hymie chose Crombie Street is its remarkably convenient location. It was about five blocks from Colfax School (where I went to grade school); and about four in the other direction from Taylor Allderdice High School from which all three of us graduated (admittedly far apart in time....Milton and Arthur were probably there at the same time, but Arthur had graduated before I entered the seventh grade). We actually had some of the same teachers and some of them like Lon Colborn (advanced Chemistry) taught Arthur and me and Miss Brennan the German teacher I think saw all three of us. Crombie Street was about eight blocks from Murray Avenue, the major shopping area (shopping in some ways dominated my mother's life, in that she had to walk to shop almost daily...more about this later) and the streetcar stop to go to Oakland, downtown or anywhere. As far as we kids were concerned one of the great joys of Crombie Street was that at the top of the hill was Beechwood Boulevard and Frick Park which had some wonderful slopes for sled riding in the winter time and was just great for playing-around-in-the-park kind of fun. Crombie Street was also not that far from the movies...an absolutely essential Saturday afternoon event. It was also walking distance (over another great hill) to the Beth Sholom Synagogue where all three of us were Bar Mitzvah and where we spent a lot of time in Hebrew School, Sunday School and attending some Services.

The Family:

It is sometimes difficult to describe family members when you haven't seen them for a very long period. What happens is that you forget their overall features and focus in on some key characteristics which are remembered either because they are tied to specific events or were so remarkable as to dominate our memory of them. The central players in our home were clearly Mary and Hymie...and I will add more about them later but introduce them here.

Mary Mankin was a truly remarkable woman...I have never known anyone like her. Intelligent, capable, prodigiously hard working, sensitive, giving, honest and fiercely loyal...were all the good things about Mary. She saw things tragically however and looked at the dark side more than most. She was loving in a way, but did not cast a really strong maternal image ...and at times I thought she didn't like me very much (after all she was already 42 when she had me and I was supposed to be a girl...she even chose a girl's name for me...Chana, which she had to change to Choni when I turned out the way I did). She probably was the source of all of our acting ability (Art's kids, Keith, etc.) and of our teaching abilities (Bobby, David and me, etc.) in that she had an incredibly accurate but acid-tinged ability to mimic her friends and especially her relatives. She could do Bertha or Cousin Rose or Aunt Esther or even Bing Crosby so well that it was spell-binding...but always with a sort of a mean twist. There was no doubt that had she gone on the stage she would have been a Sarah Bernhardt or Lillian Gish. She was strong and tough...or perhaps resilient is a better word and had as her most important goal the family.... feeding them, clothing them, caring for them in sickness and in health and making sure they got the best she could provide. I suppose that's the epitaph she would have wanted on her tombstone ...it's most of what she lived for.

Hymie on the other hand was far less fierce and much more fun-loving. For Mary life was always a tragedy about to occur...for Hymie it was a comic play, but I don't think he ever thought of himself as the central actor. He like she, worked very, very hard. Specialty Clothing Company stayed open seven days a week (closed on legal Holidays, Yom Kippur and Rosh Hashanah) and Hymie, when he was in town opened and closed it. He spent a lot of time on the road...selling clothing "wholesale" in all of the small towns in Western Pennsylvania, Ohio and West Virginia. He drove from place to place, stayed in flea bag hotels, ate funny meals (and I am sure it will be no surprise that they were not necessarily Kosher...Mary kept a strictly Kosher house...four sets of dishes...Milchig and Fleishig for both regular times and for Pesach...but Pop could escape sometimes and did!). He was a great salesman, not really a con artist but he sold his product and himself. He was a sort of Willy Lohman, doing it all "on a smile and shoeshine", but in contrast to Willie, Hymie was "well liked" by the people he sold to---it was hard not to like him. He was kind, generous, warm, gracious and fun to be with. Hymie was a gambler...he and Uncle Leonard were the two game players in the family...but Hymie loved it and was really good at it. He was a shrewd pinochle player and I grew up watching the game that took place every Saturday night at our house. I think he was as smart as Mary but perhaps less perceptive. He was however a real learner...he loved to learn new things and try new ideas. He didn't hesitate to introduce new ideas into the business, he was the first in our family to fly (in the late thirties to New York!)...he found new places to go for the hay-fever season ...Cambridge Springs (does anyone know anything about Cambridge Springs?...did anyone but me know that they had a colony of lobo wolves there?), the White Mountains in New Hampshire, Atlantic City, and only much later, Florida. Hymie enjoyed his life...he loved his wife, his kids, his business, his gambling and his vacations (to be truthful not quite in proper order...the business always came first in our family!). More about Mary, Hymie, the business and my brothers later....

Uncles, Aunts and Cousins:

This subject covers a lot of people. Mary was one of 9 children born to her father (the first two were the half-sisters, Ida and Minnie); and Hymie had 7 brothers and sisters. This group of fifteen aunts and uncles constituted the "family" ...all immigrants from Eastern Europe who came to the United States from Lithuania between about 1897 and 1914 Everyone came in through Ellis Island and carried their possessions with them. Their parents also came to this country with them, but I knew little of them...they were too old for me to remember much about (see below).

The Mankin Side:

The Mankin family came from a town called Litvonovo...I think somewhere in Lithuania, not far from Poland. Grandpa Yadidya (Julius) and Grandma Yudus (Julia) were the father and mother for this large group and exactly how they got to Pittsburgh is not known. The origin of the name Mankin is also somewhat unclear...but probably had something to do with the city of Minsk (hence we may be related to all the people named Minsky or Monsky). Once the first ones settled in and around Pittsburgh they all came there and with the exception of Goldy who presumably moved to Oklahoma City with her husband, everyone lived out their lives and raised their families near the city of Pittsburgh.

On Hymie's side the oldest was **Goldy Minsky** who lived in Oklahoma and had to the best of my knowledge, one son named **Henry**. I think that Goldy came to visit once or twice and although I have trouble recalling her I believe she was a small, bubbly woman who reminded me of Aunt Sarah. I don't recall ever meeting her husband who I understand was a cousin, hence the name, nor have I had very much knowledge of her son Henry, who I think is dead (he was considerably older than the rest of us, I believe). I think I met Henry once, but it is possible that my brothers met him more frequently.

Harry was next and he and his wife **Emma** lived in Wheeling West Virginia where they owned and operated a department store...the Peerless Department Store in the downtown area (does it still stand?...I recently asked an old timer from there and he remembered it but said that it is gone). They had one daughter, **Helen** who now lives in St. Louis. She looked a lot like the rest of the family and I remember her as being very pleasant and warm. She was Arthur's age, I believe and quite bright.

Next came Uncle **Jake** who lived in Pittsburgh, first on Dinwiddie Street and then on Forward Avenue. He was married to **Ethel** (Mary called her Die Kuh...[yiddish for cow!]) and they had two children **Bernard** (poor Bernie had some sort of autistic behavior pattern and was probably schizophrenic) and **Joan** (pronounced Jo-anne) (who was my age and to whom early on I gave the nickname Jo-animal!).

Leonard was next. He lived somewhere in East Liberty [a section of Pittsburgh] early on but then moved to Columbo Street near Stanton Avenue. He was the one who escaped from Russia to avoid being drafted into the Army during the 1914 war. He was as all knew a heavy gambler and unlike my father, I think he was often a heavy loser. He drove a truck for the United Baking Company and sometimes delivered to our home. He was fun to be with...loud, a bit coarse and I remember him coming into the house and smelling of fresh bread. Leonard was married to an irrepressible lady with real charm...my Aunt **Julie** who just loved to laugh. Together they raised three children ...**Shirley**, **Sanford** and **Gerald**, a sort of rough and tumble crew coarse and loud like their father and mother but good people and fun to be with. Gerald was the youngest cousin on this side, I believe and had a brain tumor...he survived and apparently had no deficit suggesting that it was a meningioma. Sanford lived in Pittsburgh and ran a Delicatessen there (Sandy's) but the other two and their families moved to Los Angeles.

Next came **Sarah**...a good lady who carried along with her the family intellect and capacity. She was a tiny model of the rest of her siblings (maybe five feet tall). Along with her husband **Jake** Green she lived in Butler, PA where Jake was in the junk business. They had two children, **Sidney** a year or two older than me and **Lucille** who was my age...someone that I was quite close to early in our childhood. I liked her then and still do. Sidney went to college at Duquesne and stayed at our house a lot of nights during my early teen years...when he came to the house, I often had to sleep on the day bed in the breakfast room....not so bad since I could read far into the night without my mother telling me to turn out the lights.

The youngest and most extraordinary of my father's family was **Joe** who lived in Russia during the 1917 Revolution and was an avowed Communist...really I think a Trotzkyite. Joe was the only relative I knew who lived on the North Side. He was extraordinarily bright and remarkably articulate...spouting Marxist philosophy (along with columns of cigarette smoke...he was a chain smoker) at every family gathering. He had a nice smile and an easy manner and really cared for us kids. He and **Agnes**, his common-law wife (what else would you expect from a Trotskyite!) never had children of their own (they raised cats instead). Because of Joe's constant commentary about the government and his strong identification with the Communist party, he had trouble finding work and ended up working for Uncle Israel Skirboll (my father's uncle) at his pickle factory on the North Side.

One other child in the Mankin clan was one that I never knew...her name was **Rebecca** and she was married to a fellow named Goodman. She died of cancer very early in her life and left two children, **Dorothy** and **Esther** whom I met a few times. Arthur and my cousin Lucille knew them better than I did...they ended up living in first Harrisburg, I think and then New York City or New Jersey.

The Simons Side:

Mary's family also came from Eastern Europe not far from Hymie's and we have some pictures of her from a town in Lithuania called Marienpol, not far from the Polish and East Prussian Borders. The actual town that they came from was just south of there and it like Litvonovo was a "Shtetel" [a small Jewish enclave, typically in Eastern Europe] and may have had the name of Starovno. The family name was Simonovich or some such which became anglicized to Simons shortly after arrival in the United States. According to Mary, her father and mother had a farm in the countryside with a store which served the local people and she, Mary not only worked on the farm (I am sure with the same extraordinary zeal and intensity that she displayed for the next seventy years) but also sold produce to Polish, Lithuanian, Russian and German people in the store. It was to this that she attributed her remarkable fluency in all of these languages, but it may have been her remarkable ear...she was spectacular at reproducing sounds of things like accents. I vaguely recall her father and mother but I can't really picture them and I don't know that I had any kind of contact with them.

The first two members of Mary's family to arrive in this country were Ida and Minnie who were the eldest siblings, and in fact were half-sisters to the rest (their mother died in childbirth with Minnie and their father remarried and had seven additional children!). The two girls immigrated around the turn of the century and came to live with some relatives in Buffalo or Rochester (no one has ever been' sure which city it was). The relatives were named Farber and some of them subsequently became quite famous, including Sidney Farber and two of his brothers, who were physicians and scientists in California and Boston. The Dana-Farber Cancer Institute is named for Sidney who was the pioneer oncologist at Harvard in the 50s....oddly enough he and one of his brothers converted to Catholicism! The girls lived with the Farber family for a few years, but for reasons not quite clear had a falling out and decided to leave. Ida met a young man named Lechtner and she and he moved to Erie, PA where they married and raised a family; and Minnie first went to Erie with her, but then came to Pittsburgh and ultimately married Louis Cohen and raised her family. When all the rest of the family decided to leave Lithuania somewhere around 1907-1910 (see below), they came to Pittsburgh to initially live with Minnie and then establish their own lives.

Ida lived in Erie and was widowed quite early...in fact, I don't think I ever met her husband. He was a peddler, I believe but I knew very little about him. I remember Ida chiefly because she and her daughter Mary came to Pittsburgh quite frequently and they stayed with us (where did we put her?...more about that later) or sometimes with Minnie. She was as was Minnie a blond (all the rest of the family were red-haired like Harry, Rose, Jennie or dark haired like Mary, Sam and Rachel) and quite attractive in appearance although somewhat dour in personality. I remember that she drank prodigious quantities of black coffee and also delivered some of the loudest gaseous eructations ever heard on Crombie Street! She had five children, **Robert, Mary, Bennie, Jack** and **Marvin** all of whom we saw infrequently. They occasionally came to Pittsburgh or we sometimes in the summer time or for a special event drove to Erie. Bob was a dentist and certainly the first of that generation to go to college and dental school. He was a nice man and apparently a good dentist and established a home and life for himself in Erie...with what I thought of as a story book romance with a very attractive lady name Tony from Cleveland. Mary or more appropriately as she was known in the family "Mary from Erie" was a spinster, forever trying to meet someone and was a frequent visitor to Pittsburgh, whenever someone fixed her up with a blind date. She would sometimes stay at Crombie Street for several days when she had dates or doctor's appointments and she was not an easy guest for my mother, Mary. The rest of the boys, particularly Bennie and Jack went into the shoe business and apparently did quite well. They were big and hearty and everyone liked them. Mary worked there as well. Marvin on the other hand was our family ne'er-do-well...the black sheep who was involved in some brushes with the law and some devious businesses of sort.

The next in line was **Minnie** who lived with her husband **Lou Cohen** on South Evaline Street off of Penn Avenue and not far from St. Francis Hospital in Pittsburgh. I was never sure what Louie did...he was not really very communicative (even to his children, I think!), although I recall seeing him at Specialty occasionally so I think he was in some kind of selling business. I don't think they were poor, though and as a matter of fact they may have been the wealthiest of Mary's siblings. Minnie was, as was Ida, a fabulous cook (I remember some wonderful meals in her dining room) and a vivacious woman, generous and warm. She had a very special smile which was undimmed by the years or her subsequent mental clouding. I really liked visiting her and their house…it was a special place with a porch (with a swing), fine furniture and a beautiful (but I think unused) fireplace. Their children **Bob** and **Honey** were as in the case of Ida's children, older than the rest of us and by the time I started visiting, were no longer living at home. Bob was a physician and after graduating from Pitt Medical School opened up an office on Penn Avenue...I think he was my first doctor and in fact sort of a role model. He was in the Army during World War II and upon discharge became a psychiatrist. Everyone liked his sister Honey, who was really beautiful in a "thirties sort of way". She wasn't exactly a "flapper" but she did have extraordinary grace and a low-pitched and distinctive voice...I liked watching and listening to her. One of my earliest recollections was attending a family wedding at their house when Honey married Irwin, her first husband...that must have been 1934 or so.

Unless I am mistaken, the next oldest on that side of the family was **Rose** who was everyone's Aunt Rosie. She must have been a beautiful young lady...red hair, a kind of glowing complexion and a Rubenesque figure. She was twice widowed, first from Nudler and then from Harris (both died young...when I was growing up I used to fantasize that their remains might be in two large trunks that Rose kept in the cellar at Crombie Street). She was Mary's closest friend. She at one point lived in the house (where did she sleep?...it must have been after Milton went to the Army in 1941 or 1942 and then she occupied the small bedroom). She and Mary went downtown shopping every Saturday together...to Kaufman's, Rosenbaum's, Frank and Seder, Joseph Horne and all the rest...they took me occasionally and I can still remember the ride on the 68 or 69 streetcar (we picked it up at Phillips and Murray) and after a day of shopping going to Child's restaurant for a chocolate ice-cream sundae. Rose had no children and was Aunt Rosie to all the cousins and later to the Jewish Baby's Home in

East Liberty where she was a cook for many years. My mother thought she was vain and superstitious, and I guess she was but I also thought she was very loving. She was a dreadfully fearful lady....terribly concerned about illness, injury, disasters and especially the things that could happen to children...I can vividly recall her concerns about the summers of the polio epidemics, spinal meningitis (terrifying words to her...and to everyone) and her admonitions and concerns regarding bicycle riding, sports and a host of other life's circumstances.

I think my Aunt **Rachel** was next... or "Rochke" as my mother called her. I don't remember her at all. She was married to a man named Watzman and she died of cancer at a very young age, leaving two children, **Milton** and **Robert** Watzman. Her husband remarried and had another son, Nathan but he was not in the family. Milt ("Maash") and Bob ("Boozizie"...as my father callled him) were close to us and were frequent visitors at Crombie Street in their early lives and I think at one point one or both of them lived with us, although I'm not sure whether it was at Crombie or Bluff St. Milt ended up being a lawyer and Bob was in some sort of retail business. Later in their lives they were not very involved in family activities for some odd reason, although Mary kept pretty close track of them particularly while they were still single. My brother Milton was their contemporary and didn't like them very much, I think....Milton Watzman was a bit acid and mean, but Bob was pleasant at least to me.

My uncle **Sam** was next and he was a twin...his brother died quite young and I am not sure even made it to the United States. Sam was lean and spare (and somewhat dour...did anyone ever hear Sam laugh?) and was in the trunk and bag business (see below). Sam spent a lot of time on the road and sometimes teamed up with Hymie (I think my father liked him more than Harry!). Sam was discovered to be a diabetic in his late forties and it was like all illnesses a source of worry (and conversation) to the family. It seems to me that he managed quite well and considering that this was in the thirties, it must have been rather mild disease. He and his wife **Esther** (a big woman and a good cook with a heavy accent which Mary loved to imitate!) lived on Flemington Street on the other side of the Murray Avenue bridge and had two children, **Eddie** (a pharmacist in Carnegie until recently) and **Annette**, who was almost my contemporary (she was about two years older). My mother implied many times that Annette was not a well person but I was never able to assess the nature of her illness...probably some sort of inflammatory bowel disease.

Harry Simons was next in line, I think and Mary was closest to him and his wife **Nellie**. They lived first on Eldridge Street and then on Douglas Street just a few blocks from us and we visited them frequently. Harry was a partner with his brother Sam and another person named Sam Weiner in the Reliable Trunk and Bag Company (located on Fifth Avenue not far from our beloved oldest sibling...Specialty Clothing Company!). Harry was the family cynic...he had pretty much of a bad word to say about everyone except for his wife and kids (and not always did he spare them!). He was bright, capable and irritable a lot of the time. He and his two partners spent time on the road. Aunt Rosie shared her time between Harry and Nellie's house and ours and was particularly close to Nellie (Nellie often joined Rosie and my mother on their Saturday shopping tours). Nellie also had a sister Bertha (called in the family "Breinke") to whom she was close and also a brother Sam Nowling to whom she never spoke, who also lived on Douglas Street. No one ever knew why they were so estranged. Harry and Nellie had four children. **Davy** the oldest was a contemporary of Milt's and was "in the business"; **Marcella** (forever known to the family and all of her friends as "Tootsie") who was a year or two younger than Arthur was also "in the business" and in fact eventually ended up owning it for a time; **Gerald** (a year or two older than me) lived in Florida and New York for a while; and **Mortie**, who was not then or ever an easy person to live with...I don't think anyone liked him very much. This branch of the family collected unusual illnesses...Gerald and Mortie both had to have mastoid surgery and Gerald had St. Vitus Dance [Sydenham's chorea – a self-limited but recurrent convulsive disease]. (I think I first met him when he was in bed at their home on Eldridge Street recovering from an episode!).

The last of Mary's siblings was **Jennie** who lived in New York City with her husband **Max** Korman. Jennie was the youngest and probably the fairest of the Simons girls...she was really quite beautiful, although according to my mother, not very smart. She however was bright enough to marry her husband who was a very intelligent, energetic and enthusiastic man. Max sold furniture in east Harlem and much of his talent was "Schlock Salesmanship"... a very special technique that my father and indeed all of the men in the wholesale or retail business had to have. They lived in the Bronx and had four nice children. I remember meeting them quite early in my life (I don't think I was yet 6) and liking **Sally** (the oldest), **Jerry**, **Richard** and my favorite, **Annabelle**, about my age and whom I promptly nicknamed Annabear (a name that stuck throughout her short and unfortunately unhappy life). She was the sweetest and nicest of my cousins I think. I can remember staying with them when Mary, Hymie and I went to the New York World's Fair [1939]...what a great time for me...and Annabear!

So, that's the lot of them. With my mother and father included, there were a total of 16 Simons and Mankins who emmigrated from Eastern Europe in the first decade of the century... who lived, visited or were somehow intertwined with us during those early years at Crombie Street; and if you add in their spouses, there were a total of 26 in that generation. Our generation consisted of 33 members, all born in the United States, between 1910 and around 1934. Milton, Arthur and I found that we belonged to a rather closely knit cuzship mostly living in western Pennsylvania. Some of the 59 members of this cast of characters, like Aunt Rosie played a major role in our growing up; while others were quite peripheral or scarcely ever involved. And, as one might expect, there aren't that many left now.

Brothers and Friends:

As can be clearly understood from the family constellation, mine was almost surely an unwanted pregnancy. Arthur is 7 years older than I am and Milton 12 and my mother was 42 years of age when she had me. She once told me that she was embarassed to be pregnant at that age so wore a tight corset until almost the end of term in order to conceal the fact. She had her share of tight corsets since she had once been diagnosed as having a "floating kidney" and needed to support that by wearing specially made garments with heavy stays...and in fact, she was never without her garment in those early days except late in the day (I think the best part about wearing it was how good it must have felt when she took it off!). Anyway, she wore it during my intrauterine time and I think I still bear some marks (of one sort or another!). The only way It was tolerable to have a child at this age was if it was a girl (Milton and Arthur being males) and she decided early in the pregnancy that that's what I was. As I indicated above she gave me a girl's name, Chana (Hannah in English) later reluctantly changed to Choni which was anglicized or translated into Henry (incidentally, an odd name for a Jewish family...I don't know very many Henrys and even fewer Jewish ones!).

Anyway, there I was entering the world in 1928, with a 7 year old brother and a 12 year old one. We now lived on Crombie Street and I began to grow up in the world I have described in part above. My brothers helped me a lot, I think...they not only tolerated me (what you might expect from two so much older siblings) they taught me many things. Arthur taught me how to play chess (Milton taught him a few years before) and about stamps (in fact I more or less inherited his stamp collection when he left home ...and still have it!), to ice skate (I never really learned) and most importantly to read. He himself was a voracious reader and made me the same, perhaps even more so. Milton taught me to swim, to sing (such as I do!) and passed on to me his mother's wish that one of us play the violin (with the identical disastrous result...I am afraid to the eternal distress of Mary, the Mankin males are not able to master this traditional form of Jewish musicianship...Alas!). In different ways they served as role models for me...and the reason for that is obvious...they were really quite different.

Milton was a really quite beautiful child and a handsome young man. He was graceful, charming and articulate. He perhaps more than Arthur and I resembled his mother...Arthur and I looked a lot more like Hymie. He was a bit vain and in fact was somewhat egotistical, I think. He was one of the few of the cousins that went to college (Pitt) but didn't achieve his lifelong desire (or was it Mary's?) that he enter Medical School and become a physician. Although he became a dentist during the war he never really practiced. He was also the brother who was inducted into the military during World War II which had an enormous effect on his outlook and materially changed his life.

Milton made friends easily and was the center figure in a crowd of 30's teenagers who in a measured way, tested the limits of social constraint for the time. He smoked, sang with a dance band, dressed beautifully and with great concern for details, dated a host of very attractive women, frequented the dance halls and road houses of the day returning to Crombie Street late almost every night; and to Mary's consternation was almost impossible to rouse every morning. He worked at Specialty Clothing Company after completing college and because of his interest in numbers and figures (he had a real talent for organization of data) soon took over the business aspect of the store, leaving much of the sales to the others. He tried going out on the road a few times, didn't like it and stayed inside from then on. He was a warm and caring person who was a bit weaker than some of the other figures in the family but perhaps was more of a victim of the times than they were. I never doubted that he loved me and I in turn adored him.

Arthur was different. My mother always implied that he was a "roshi"...a headstrong and difficult person who did things that made the family uncomfortable. I never saw him that way. He was for me, a teacher. He was much more scholarly than Milton and was talented in math and science. He was one of Lon Colborn's early chemistry prodigies at Taylor Allderdice High School and I don't know whether he was first in his class, but should have been. He was not nearly as social as Milton for reasons not clear to me and although he had a coterie of friends they were chess-players or fellow scholars rather than social gads-about. He didn't dress with the same panache as Milton nor did he care that much about his appearance (a trait which extended through his entire life). Arthur frequently needed a haircut (Milton never did!) and often didn't wear a tie to family events. Arthur thought more deeply about things than Milton did and he embraced some causes with the same intensity that my Uncle Joe (the Communist!) did. As I indicated above, he read incessantly and omnivorously...including history, poetry, fiction, science and whatever. He clearly knew a lot of things and when I needed to either know something or how to find it, Arthur was a wonderful source. He did irritate my mother some...and I guess more often had to be "talked to" by Hymie when he came home than Milton or me. Arthur entered the University of Pittsburgh graduated and was probably the very first of the cousins to leave home in pursuit of an education...he went to graduate school at the University of Minnesota.

Arthur's relationship to his brothers was complex. As I indicated his intensity and intellectual approach made communication more difficult and he far more then Milton challenged the status of things and statements about them. He didn't really get along all that well with Milton...I don't think they fought, but they were not really friends and didn't do much together. He, I suspect was closer to me, but not by much and he sometimes made me feel uncomfortable about not achieving enough or knowing enough. I on the other hand revered his knowledge and his capacity...and modeled much of my academic career after him. I tried to learn like he did and even went so far as to be a Physics major at Pitt before entering Medical School. Despite the discomfort that he occasionally aroused by his challenges, Arthur was really my academic role model and I attribute my success in these settings to the things I learned from him.

I had a few friends on Crombie Street in those early days. My first best friend (about the age of four or so) was my next door neighbor, Myron Kopelman. He was about 6 months younger than I was and a little smaller. He lived at 6309 (slightly smaller than our house) with his father and mother and a pair of twin sisters (Violet and Marie) and another sister, Shirley and we played in the back yards. Those who know Pittsburgh radio will recognize that he became Myron Cope...a famous local sports announcer and commentator. Next door to them at 6311 were the Sauls and Rogals. Mr. and Mrs. Saul had a daughter Minnie whose husband, Joe Rogal was in the ladies ready to wear business. They had one child...a daughter named Selma who was about a year older than me and Myron. She was a "tomboy" (aren't most girls at that age?) and she joined us in play in the back yards but had her own friends and entered school earlier than we did.

Across the street were two families that moved in somewhat later (I can remember them building the house!). The male member of that family constellation was Leroy Weiner, who I was very close to for most of my formative years. Leroy was the son of Sam and Mollie Weiner who were in the trunk and bag business with my uncles Sam and Harry but soon dropped out to start their own, much more successful enterprise. He, his mother and father and his sister Dorothy (Milton's age) and Jay (a few years older than Leroy and I) all lived in the first floor of a two family house. On the second story was the first "love interest" that I had...Leroy's cousin Hermoine Rubin. I couldn't have been more than 9 when I decided that she was wonderful and that I would even tolerate her tag-along kid sister Eileen for an opportunity to go to the movies with her...I never did! Leroy moved away (he later died of disseminated lymphoma at an early age) and I remember seeing Hermoine some years later (she stayed beautiful) but I don't know what happened to either her or her sister Eileen.

All of us went to Colfax school where we started in Kindergarten together and then went through the sixth grade. The principal at the time was Hedwig Pregler (the first and I think the last person I ever knew with that first name). She was special in that she taught us how to read, perhaps more effectively than had ever been done previously and placed emphasis on our ability to extend our horizons through the printed pages. I remember the first "grown-up" book that I read was Kipling's Jungle Book and this was followed by the Dr. Doolittle series...Oh, how I loved them! I was left handed (as was Arthur) and she spared me the need to learn to write with my right hand. I think we may have been the first class to do that...but I do remember having considerable trouble making those circles for the Palmer method [of cursive penmanship] with my left hand. Another very memorable thing about Colfax school was the Cua Brothers store across the street. It was run by an aged couple, Mr. and Mrs. Cua and they had the most extraordinary collection of penny candy in the world.

I have no trouble remembering some of my classmates in those early days but there are none who became lasting friends. I know who they are and occasionally hear of them or even from them and can recall some of those days and those events. I do remember however somewhere around the mid-thirties meeting new children at Colfax with accents and strange hand writing who were immigrants from Europe trying to escape Hitler's purge of the Jews. It was my first knowledge of the European holocaust which occurred over the next ten years and killed six million of our people.

Specialty Clothing Company:

I have already tipped my hand by referring to Specialty Clothing Company, Hymie's business as being our "oldest and most beloved sibling" and I don't think you would get much of an argument from Milton, Arthur or me or indeed anyone who knew us. Hymie started life as a peddler...he quickly learned the language and the tricks of selling. He became extraordinarily good at it and became a star clothing salesman for a firm called Abels and Ress. Shortly after he married Mary, he was approached by Samuel Karelitz, a man with some money but limited business ability who proposed starting a business together. They agreed and Specialty Clothing Company, "wholesalers and retailers of men's and boy's clothing" was born. Hymie as could be anticipated was the driving force in the business. He did it all. He bought the merchandise from salesmen from the New York manufacturers (including such household words for us at the time as Joseph H. Cohen and Sons) either there or here; took the heavy sample cases out on the road every week beginning on Monday, sold in the store on Friday afternoon, Saturday and Sunday...and then off again on the next Monday. It wasn't much of a life for him...or for us, I guess but it certainly established a model in all our minds for the work ethic. Karelitz was shy and not very knowledgeable but stayed inside. In later years, he was joined by his son Hymie Karelitz, who was Milton's contemporary and I suspect that there was some rivalry between the two. Hymie bought out the Karelitz part of the business during or right after the war, I think.

The business was located at 919-921 Fifth Avenue, in a district known as Uptown (to be distinguished from Downtown where the Department Stores were). It was a wholesale district and on all sides of us there were wholesalers of ladies ready to wear (Seiner and Colker), hosiery (Tanur Bros), trunks and bags (the Reliable Trunk and Bag...Harry and Sam's business), sporting goods (A. L. Robbins), shirts (Reidbord Bros) and other men's clothing stores, including especially our arch rivals...Wolk Brothers across the street and Morgan and Kaufman just two doors away.

Our store was pretty spartan at first with windows to show off the latest styles but not much inside but the clothing and a few chairs to sit in. The original Specialty had no frills...pipe racks with men's clothing on wooden hangers arranged by style and size with rather phenomenally low prices even for the depression days. We sold blue serge suits with two pairs of pants for under $15.00, heavy overcoats for about the same and separate pants for under $3.00 (in many cases including alterations). A business office was about halfway back on the left side and was the home of the one female member on the staff (the first I remember was a Miss Pitler although shortly after I started working in the store the acid tongued Dorie Berger replaced her...and a string of them followed after that). There was some space in the back for some tailoring although initially most of our alteration work was sent out to Harry the Tailor around the corner on Washington Street (under the Washington Trust Company where we did our banking). The store was not terribly well lit, nor did it have an efficient heating system for the winter...and of course air conditioning was unknown yet. The most modern thing we had in addition to the adding machine and typewriter was a water cooler with a large bottle of water which sat on an icebox, filled daily by the iceman.

Business varied a good bit from season to season. The clothing merchants old joke comes to mind: "In the men's clothing business there are five seasons...the fifth being the slack season"...our slack season was the summer. It seems like at times no one came in for days at end. Hymie and Mary routinely took off the last two weeks in August to get away from the ragweed (his hay fever was prodigious and despite his weekly shots to be desensitized, he sneezed his way through late August until the blessed first frost). Busy times at Specialty came with Back to School (not too big), Christmas (big) and especially Easter (very big....called by Sam Goldberg the "Easter Rush") and I am not exactly sure why. Not that many people marched in an Easter parade and in fact, I am not really sure that there was one in Pittsburgh [the annual St. Patrick's Day Parade was considered an "Easter Rising" event, but there is no record of a traditional Pittsburgh Easter parade]...but in any event everyone needed a new suit for Easter and everyone in the family (Hymie, Mary, Milton, Arthur and even me) had to work.

The employees of Specialty were as unique as the store itself. Sam Goldberg was Hymie's oldest employee...a former tailor turned salesperson. He was a good person and a fine salesman (admittedly with a rather heavy hand). It was said of Sam that he once sold a suit with two pairs of pants to an undertaker for a body ... clearly an apocryphal story, but probably not far off, since I am sure he tried! Sam was loyal and clever...not really a great business man (Hymie was a business man) but he knew how to sell and what would sell and Hymie depended on him for that. Ike (Casey) Kessler was also a loyal and hardworking salesman. A string of road men come to mind...Bennie Horowitz, Jack Myers and some Sunday helpers Izzy Karelitz (a cousin of the original part owner), Jake Magedoff and a lot of others. They worked long hours at Specialty Clothing Company and presumably were paid reasonably well for it, but even if they didn't like it (or like Hymie...although most of them did) it was the depression and the job was steady and payed even when other people were on breadlines.

Almost as important as the store itself were the three restaurants on Uptown Fifth Avenue...all three delicatessens of very special cuisine. Al Rice's was the closest...it was across the street next to Wolk Brothers and served good sandwiches mostly at a counter with a few tables and a very busy pool room in the back. Betting on numbers and shooting pool for money was a not so occasional pastime for Hymie and his friends, when he was in town. Across Washington Street and further uptown was Goldstein's Restaurant, a bit more formal with more sit-down space and even further up near Dinwiddie and Tisherman's bakery (a landmark) and Fifth Avenue High School (Milton started there and then transferred to Allderdice) was Richest's Delicatessen... probably the "haut cuisine" of the avenue. It was really a special treat to go to Richests for lunch...a privilege I didn't have very often.

So that was my oldest sibling...It was subsequently remodelled several times, given to Milton when Hymie retired, then willed to Cecille at Milton's death, and she sold it to Larry Rubin. Although the name still exists it is obviously very different. I can still remember the way it was...the irregular floor boards under my feet, making boxes at a scarred table in the back, the smell of wool clothing, the cracks in the plaster wall, Miss Pitler's electric heater during the winter, the unisex bathroom next to the dressing room...I can even remember the phone number.... Atlantic 8284! I am amazed at how clear the picture remains after all these years.

Entertainment at Crombie Street:

What did we do for entertainment in the early and middle thirties? I guess it varied with the individuals and was probably very much age-related. My father was into pinochle and virtually every Saturday night there was a game at Crombie Street. I don't remember all the players...just a few like Doc Lewin and Benny Horowitz ...those were serious games...we were allowed to watch but could not comment. Mary was a surprisingly good bridge player and played often in the evenings with Aunt

Nellie and some of their friends. She didn't play much after the war, I don't know why.

I think the universal entertainment was the radio. A large old standup Majestic stood in the living room and I can remember sitting and listening as late as Mary would let me. I remember some of the evening programs: Mr. First Nighter, Jack Benny, One Man's Family, Major Bowes Amateur Hour, The Goldbergs, The Guiding Light and when they would let me stay up on Saturday night...the Lucky Strike Hit Parade and Lights Out, a show that absolutely terrorized me.

One thing that we all did (Arthur and I led the pack) was read...there really wasn't a lot else to do...but it wasn't boredom that made me read...I loved it. I read prodigiously and in fact omnivorously. I took books out of the Colfax Library, read Arthur's books (one of the first paper backs was his...Ellery Queen's "The Chinese Orange Mystery"). When I found out about Carnegie Library and could go by streetcar by myself, I went every Saturday and not only browsed but took out four or five books to read at home. I started with children's books and rapidly graduated to Mark Twain, Kipling, Conan Doyle, Dickens and then mysteries. I read my school books as well, but really learned about the world and lived out all my fantasies over the printed pages. I don't know what I would have done without them!

Movies were the real entertainment and everyone participated. Mary would occasionally take me to the movies but when I got to be old enough to go by myself or with one of the neighbor kids (Myron Kopelman who lived next door or Leroy Weiner or Sonny Gottlieb who lived across the street) Saturday afternoon was the movie day. The Manor Theatre on Murray and Darlington was the oldest and certainly the largest theatre in the neighborhood; but the Squirrel Hill opened up soon into the thirties. The Beacon was the last to open and that was in the late thirties or early forties. The Squirrel Hill was my favorite. It was located on

Forward Avenue, just up from Murray Avenue. Every Saturday, they had a double feature with short subjects almost invariably, at least two serials (Flash Gordon or Zorro, etc.) and news and sometimes a travelogue or some such. Mary would give me twenty-five cents....ten cents to get into the movie, five cents for a package of Good and Plenty Candy, ten cents for a hot dog and a Pepsi at the Hot Puppy Shop down the street afterwards. What a treat!

I don't recall ever going to movies outside of Squirrel Hill in those days, although I think on occasion Mary and Aunt Rosie would take me to a movie downtown on one of our Saturday shopping expeditions. As far as music was concerned Milton and I both took violin lessons (all for naught) and Milton really had a pretty good singing voice. I don't recall that the family ever went to a concert in those early days. Pittsburgh had stage shows at places like the Stanley Theatre (Dick Powell was a crooner there in the thirties) and had legitimate theatre at the Nixon, but the Mankins never went as far as I recall. There was however Kennywood Park...an amusement park with a Ferris wheel and lots of rides for tiny kids and also for grownups. It was located at the end of the 68 streetcar line. We would go there sometimes, the whole family to celebrate the fourth of July and for those occasions Mary would pack a big picnic basket. That was good fun and very exciting.

The most entertaining things that we all did, however were family visits. We would visit Nellie and Harry (Harry and my father would play cards while the ladies talked and I played with Gerald or the miserable Mortie); or Ethel, Jake, Bernard and Joan would come to our house for an evening; or we would go to Sam and Esther's house for a meal. Trips to South Evaline Street to see Minnie were fun and the real excitement was a long drive in the car to Erie...we didn't do that very often, though. The family also visited each other on Holidays, mostly Jewish ones, so that we could always expect someone to come to our house to break the fast after Yom Kippur or come for Purim to taste Mary's homantashen (not so tasty...see below). Perhaps the greatest and most entertaining series of events were family celebrations ...mostly happy ones like bar mitzvahs (every male cousin had one!) or weddings (I remember the singing and dancing quite vividly when Honey Cohen was married); and, despite the somber nature of the visit, even paying condolence calls to people sitting Shivah when someone in the family died was a source of family entertainment.

By today's standards, it was a time of limited opportunity for entertainment...radio was in its early days and television didn't exist. I, at least, lived vicariously in the printed pages and I think lots of others did. It was the depression and although things didn't cost very much, no one had any money. We couldn't afford vacations (except for Hymie's annual seasonal attempt to escape the cursed ragweed and golden rod) and most of the entertainment was heavily family-oriented....fortunately, the family was for the most part highly entertaining! It was clearly a different time but as I look back a happy one...I don't remember any really bad times and there were lots of good ones.

The Synagogue and "Yiddishkeit":

As most everyone who will read this knows, the Jews from Eastern Europe (Ashkenazi) are divided into three basic religious groups. Those who practiced the first of these, **Orthodoxy**, adhered to a strict religious protocol and dietary code and attended highly structured Services. The Synagogue (in this case the Poale Zedek on Shady and Phillips Avenues, one block from Crombie Street) was central in their lives and there was little time left for outside things. Orthodox Jews (not to be confused with Hassidim who dress differently and have a different set of customs and codes) wore skull caps, strictly kept the Sabbath, attended Services two or three

times a day and many were Talmudic or Bible scholars. The second group, the **Conservatives** (to which all the Mankins and Simons belonged), payed considerably less attention to the Jewish laws and had a more secular outlook. Although all the boys were Bar Mitzvah (the Bat Mitzvah for girls had not become prevalent yet) and went to Hebrew School (every weekday afternoon, except Friday from 4:30 to 6:00) and
often to Saturday Services, there was far less formality to the religious experience and considerably less time required. We did not wear skull caps (yarmulkies as they were called) outside of the Synagogue, did not attend morning (Schachris), afternoon (Minchoh) or evening (Maariv) Services (except when we were in our obligate period of mourning for a deceased relative), could ride and even work on the Sabbath (as did Mary and Hymie and most of our uncles and cousins) and few of us were serious Hebrew scholars. The **Reformed** Jews didn't have a Synagogue...the went to a Temple and held short, not very ritualistic Services with limited exposure to either Hebrew or what I call "Yiddishkeit". The nearest reformed Temple to Squirrel Hill and Crombie Street was the Rodef Sholom on Fifth Avenue in Shadyside (same Fifth Avenue as Specialty was on but further east past the University).

Our Synagogue or "Shule" as we called it was the Beth Sholom at the corner of Beacon Street and Shady Avenue and it was a large and quite imposing structure (or maybe I was small when I first saw it!). It was founded in 1917 and in the thirties it was still relatively new. The main Sanctuary where the Torahs were kept was large and unlike the Orthodox services in which women were separated from the men, the families all sat together. Friday night and Saturday (Shabbas) Services were actually quite pleasant, in that the Cantor (Chazan) a man named Tolochko had a very good voice and the liturgical Hebrew chants of the Sabbath Service at least then were melodious and in some parts quite beautiful. We had the first choir in the mid-thirties prior to the time of my bar mitzvah and that made it even better, but most of our music was initially solo and a cappella. Our Rabbi was named Goodman A. Rose and he was an imposing figure. His sermons were serious commentary on the times and by and large he was a "no-nonsense" Rabbi...stern but fair and thorough.

Rosh Hashanah (The New Year) was an exciting holiday for us with a spirit of gaiety, the blowing of the Shofar (the ram's horn), more joyous music and some parading around. I remember how dressed up the congregation was (my Mother used to call it "farputzt"). In Pittsburgh Gentiles bought their new clothes for Easter while the Jews did it for Rosh Hashanah! Yom Kippur was somber...the Day of Atonement...sort of a mass confession...and we all fasted (kids for only half a day but everyone else all day). Every year, someone fainted at the Service.

Perhaps the best holiday was Pesach (Passover) which lasted about 10 days and at which we had at least two and in the early days four feasts called Seders (two at the beginning and two at the end). The ceremony commemorates the flight of the Jews from Egypt to Palestine and Moses bringing down the 10 Commandments. It was really a scene at Crombie Street. We usually had at least 10 people at the Seders and although Hymie read the Hagodah rapidly, it still took almost 3 hours from start until we ate. As most people know there are several glasses of wine that are consumed during the description of the trip across the Red Sea and defining the plagues, etc. and all the rest and the kids slowly got quieter and more flushed as the evening wore on. I think I had to be carried to bed several times during those early days. Mary of course changed dishes for Passover and we ate Matzohs...not only directly but in the form of Matzoh balls in our soup, Matzoh Brie (a rather exotic eggy dish with pancake syrup), and Matzoh and eggs for breakfast, etc.

Adjacent to the Beth Sholom Synagogue was our Hebrew School in which we were all somewhat reluctantly enrolled from age 8 until Bar Mitzvah. Although there were a number of other figures in the program Mr. Emmanuel Baradon was the principal and ruled with an iron hand. He was very knowledgeable and quite capable but frightened some of his young subjects with a perpetual glower that occupied his face. He wasn't a bad person...he just looked like a bad person! He had a son and a daughter-in-law who both taught in the Hebrew and Sunday schools and I had far less trouble with both of them. I think everyone was frightened of Mr. Baradon and also Mr. Abe Caplan...who was President of the Congregation...and looked like what I imagined the Beadle looked like in Oliver Twist. We learned our Hebrew though, but never enough to do more than stumble through our Haftorah and our prayers...and each one of us did. We actually had a Bar Mitzvah Club which met on Sunday morning to learn how to lay Tefillin amongst other things and were served a hearty breakfast by the members of the Sisterhood (my mother belonged!).

Another aspect of our Yiddish heritage were the ceremonies associated with death. Death in the Jewish family and community was a major event and had a whole series of associated rituals. First was the fact of early burial without embalming so that unless death occurred on Shabbas (one could not be buried on the Sabbath) burial occurred on the following day. It was to the funeral parlor the night before to view the body (and most often that was Ralph Schugar's in the East End or Blank Brothers in Oakland) and then off to the Beth Sholom Cemetery In Millvale The procession was long and the ceremony was even longer It seemed to me...and all the rituals such as having the black tie cut (rending of clothing), washing hands before entering the family house (an old plague prevention, I think), eating eggs as the first meal (symbolic of a dedication to life); and visiting the family of the deceased during Shivah ...a full week of mourning in the family home. The mirrors were all covered in the Shivah house (no vanity!) and the family sat on low seats or stools (to emphasize their humility). Neighbors brought food and the family sat and talked far into the night...a really remarkable way of distracting the mourners...and really quite effective.

Just a word about Yiddishkeit. All of us were proud of being Americans as were our parents, but old habits and patterns disappear slowly. We were raised in Yiddish tradition...the boys at least for a time lay Tefillin (putting on the phylacteries each morning); we said the Hamotzi (prayer for breaking bread) when we started a meal; spoke Yiddish with our parents (but never with each other!); kissed the Mezuzah when we entered a room; never tasted ham or bacon or shrimp or those other forbidden things that seemed so wonderful; and defended ourselves when the kids from Greenfield or St. Philomena attacked us simply because we were Jewish (that was when I first learned that not everyone was going to love me!). It is not that we adopted Yiddishkeit willingly or even chose it by rational decision, it is just that there seemed to be nothing else for us. Furthermore, it was oddly comfortable compared with what we imagined to be the more formal life of the Gentile where people wore coats and ties to dinner!

Shopping for Food and Meals on Crombie Street:

Shopping was never easy in the early days at Crombie Street, partly because really early we had an ice-box (literally an box full of ice) and it wasn't until I was five or six that we got our first refrigerator (a Frigidaire!). So, it meant having to bring food in almost daily particularly when five, six or more of us were eating. We needed a bread man to deliver the bread (Uncle Leonard for a while) and a produce man, at first a fellow who was called "Borabear" (some sort of Russian name, I think...he was a big fellow with a heavy beard) and later Marcus who came three days a week. We also had a milk man who came bringing Otto Cream Top Milk and also butter, cream cheese and sometimes eggs. But all of that wasn't enough....Mary still had to go to Murray Avenue almost every day for all the rest. To get there she had to walk to Phillips Avenue and then down Phillips to Murray and then up Murray to the stores. It was not so bad that way, but coming back up the Phillips Avenue hill between Murray and Shady with shopping bags made it difficult for her. At the time she already had really remarkably large varicose veins and I am amazed that she didn't have more trouble with her lower extremities than she did.

Shopping on Murray Avenue involved a series of stops at the grocery (Hymie Glick ran a grocery store...not really a supermarket but it had a lot of canned goods...Mary looked carefully for the U with the circle around it on the can indicating that the contents were Kosher), at the poultry store (where the Schachat killed the chicken or pullet (or duck for special occasions) in a manner carefully proscribed by the Laws of Kashruth), the produce store which had fresh fruits and vegetables and at the meat market where only Kosher segments of beef, veal or lamb were sold. Mary thought that lamb chops were my favorite and bought them frequently...but also liked veal chops (more to eat) at least until my fifth year when I developed appendicitis about 5 hours after eating veal chops (the resultant aversion was so strong that to this day, I still have trouble eating them!). Baked goods fresh out of the oven came from Herman's Bakery at Phillips and Murray, fish from the Fish Store run by a fellow named Harry and a little later in our lives, corned beef, pastrami, tongue and peppermeat came from the Hebrew National Delicatessen, run by the Polonsky family.

Mary bought things in small quantities even after she had the refrigerator (it was always called a "Fridgidaire" even when it came from Westinghouse or wherever), partly I suppose because she didn't like to waste food (she was remarkable that way...and I think she never threw anything out!), and partly because the walk up the hill with full shopping bags could not have been easy for her. But I really think the major reason was because she really enjoyed the scene on Murray Avenue. I did too. It was exciting. Murray Avenue was colorful and exotic. It was alive with people talking to each other in foreign languages and one could taste of sights and smells unlike any other it seemed to me. I later found out, that these findings were not unique but highly characteristic of a Jewish neighborhood...sort of the way I later imagined the lower east side of New York or Whitechapel Street in London must have seemed a few years prior to that. It was fun to be there and I tried to go with her as often as I could.

Eating at Crombie Street could not by most standards be considered a gastronomic adventure....in fact let the truth be known, although my mother's sisters and sisters-in-law were good cooks, Mary didn't exactly make it into the Michelin Guide. She pretty much did the same thing every week. We had fish on Tuesday (fresh fish was bought from the fish man on Monday....never shop for fish on Sunday...it can't be fresh!). Sometime in the middle of the week we would have some sort of meat dish, usually pot-roast, occasionally lamb chops or the dreaded veal chops. When Milton was home she made him his favorite "chollant" (I would tell you what is in it...if I knew!). Sunday was soup-meat day and Hymie really loved it...with lots of salt. We also had some traditional soups...chicken, green pea and one of my favorites, lentil soup (always better on the second, third day or later). But the real mainstay of our diet over the years was chicken. Twice a week, rain or shine we would have chicken. Every Friday night, we had the traditional Jewish dinner consisting of chicken soup, broiled chicken, vegetables, usually baked potatoes (over done!) and some sort of dessert (see below!). One other night we had chicken, sometimes leftovers (nothing was ever thrown out!). Saturday night was pick-up more or less....Mary didn't like to cook on Saturday, chiefly because she and Aunt Rosie were in town shopping all day...but she also used the pretense for what it was worth, that one didn't cook on the Sabbath!. So we had either left overs (early days when we were really poor!) or cold-cuts (corned beef, tongue, pastrami, peppermeat) with rye bread and dill pickles...a real treat for the kids...and not too much in dishes for Mary. We had to have dinner over by 8:00 PM when the pinochle game commenced....and the kids started listening to the radio or whatever.

Mary was not the best cook in the world. She tended to overcook things and sometimes went to what seemed almost great lengths to ruin a piece of meat. She would broil meat to a frazzle and sometimes take a very good steak and make it into pot roast (thus feeding more people, I guess). Fish was sometimes fried but often boiled and well done. Her vegetables were forgettable and her soups although fairly tasty were made with chicken fat so that the there was always a yellow ring around the outside of the soup. Her lentil soup was special though as were her matzoh balls or noodles in chicken soup (I have to admit that during Passover each year, I had a matzoh ball lodged somewhere between my stomach and my cecum and it took almost two weeks of eating Homatz (food not kosher for Passover) to get it out!).

Desserts were mostly canned fruit (she liked to open a can of Dole pineapple slices and give everyone two slices!) and her very own special cookies. She made them on a cookie plate with a special low salt, low fat, high sugar dough and then cut them with a cookie cutter to make five-pointed stars. After baking for an appropriate length of time the cookies were stored in glass jars in the pantry where they were available to all and sundry. She made a fairly tasty set of pies, apple being her best (a bit dry by the second or third day) and lemon meringue her worst particularly when it became sort of soggy and tired after the first day or so. One of her best things though was honey cake which stayed moist a surprising length of time and had raisins and nuts in it. I liked her honey cake and I don't know anyone who has made it that well since.

All in all, even at the height of the depression, we ate well. Mary wasted very little food and no matter how little was left on the serving plate it was put away...only to later reappear in an altered form. Indeed, left-overs were an important part of our diet. Portions were small when she dished them out, but there were always seconds. Breakfast was not very often a heavy meal and mostly consisted of a bowl of Wheaties, etc. and sometimes some coffee cake or cinnamon buns from the bakery. Lunch at home (I always came home for lunch...we only lived 5-10 minutes away from school) was a sandwich or a can of spaghetti and one her cookies or some honey cake. Supper was the big meal and occurred as soon as it got dark or on days when Hymie was home when he arrived from Specialty (the store closed at 6:00 PM so we usually ate at 6:30 or so). It was possible to have something before bed...Arthur liked salami sandwiches (this brought a frown on Mary's face) but I liked a piece of honey cake and milk or some such.

We were exhorted never to leave anything on our plates and indeed made to feel enormous guilt when we did...I can still hear the words "think of the starving children in Europe". A few years ago, we had as a guest speaker at the Massachusetts General Hospital Zvi Yossipovitch, a Professor of Orthopaedics from Tel Aviv. Zvi is my age and Romanian who was growing up outside of Bucharest while I was sitting at Mary's table on Crombie Street. I couldn't resist introducing him as the reason why I was fat ...because he, Zvi was one of those starving children of Europe, the memory of which makes me feel guilty to this day if I don't "clean my plate".

Doctors, Illnesses and Medical Stuff:

The time that I am writing about was 1933 to 1938 and if I am to write appropriately about the medical picture as I and my family saw it, I have to set the background of what diseases and their treatments were like in those days. Most discoveries in medicine occur in relation to need and wars create great need ....and so it was for physicians and scientists who during World War I learned much about trauma and its management, psychiatric disorders and infectious disease. By standards of today, however, the knowledge base was rudimentary regarding the cause and diagnosis of disorders and the treatment for most was inadequate and in some cases irrational.

Childhood diseases ran rampant and unchecked...and we all had them. Measles, German measles, mumps, chicken pox were customary for all of us but fortunately we had learned to vaccinate against the dreaded smallpox so none of us were at risk (although none of us were enthusiastic about the vaccination, which left a broad scar usually on the outer aspect of the non-dominant shoulder). Tuberculosis remained a major threat. We had good radiographic imaging at the time (Roentgen's great discovery was a scant 30 or so years before) and between that and the tuberculin skin test (we all had to have it) it was possible to make the diagnosis of TB with relative ease. No drugs were as yet available however, and the only treatment at the time was isolation in a sanitarium (such as Leech Farm in Pittsburgh) and some manipulations of the pleural spaces (such as thoracoplasty or pneumoperitoneum, etc....none worked very well). Things were not a lot different in Europe in 1935 when reported by Thomas Mann in his *Magic Mountain* (another book that I read early in my life). Tuberculosis remained unchecked and always a threat. Fortunately the disease is rare in Jews and the only person who may have had it (and it is hardly clear) was Aunt Rosie at an early age.

45

Other infectious diseases were frightening. The diagnosis of bacterial diseases was accurate for most disorders and at the time such recently introduced technology as pasteurization of milk materially reduced the number of cases of typhoid fever or brucellosis. Antibiotics had not made the scene as yet and infections with staphylococcus, pneumococcus and bowel organisms if rampant could not be easily checked. Little could be done medically to aid an individual who developed a widespread septic process. Thus pneumonia had a high mortality rate (depending on the organism, over 50%) as did osteomyelitis (about 30%) and peritonitis from a ruptured appendix (over 50%). Virtually everyone died or was severely brain damaged by meningococcal meningitis.

Perhaps the most fearsome of the infectious diseases was polio. If a figure such as President Roosevelt (the only President I knew of until after the war!) could get it than anyone could. Annually in the summer in Pittsburgh, seemingly in relation to the use of the public swimming pools during the height of the heat waves, large numbers of cases of the disease broke out and some of the kids in our class disappeared only to reappear some 6 months later with braces and flaccid muscles in the arms and legs.

None of our family developed polio but my cousins Mortie and Gerald Simons both had mastoiditis and required surgery and my cousin Lois Skirboll had a distal femoral osteomyelitis and had some permanent disability and was never able to run. At the age of five I had appendicitis and was operated on at the Montefiore Hospital. I was alleged to have had a "touch" of peritonitis and was quite ill for a while requiring intravenous feeding through a cut-down over the ankle.

The diagnosis and management of coronary artery disease was fairly well established by this time and the cardiologists of the day in Pittsburgh had lots of experience with my father's family. All of them had coronary artery disease of sorts and Harry, Jake and Leonard died before the age of 50 of what must have been coronary occlusion. Hymie was spared because he unlike the others was hypotensive and didn't smoke much. He had had angina and coronary artery disease from the early 1950s on but survived to the age of 82. Even Milton who died of the same affliction at the age of 54 was a heavy smoker for much of his life but was not hypertensive. He came close to surviving in that he died just at the beginning of the era of coronary bypass surgery which might well have been very helpful to his condition. Strokes were prevalent then as were peripheral artery disease but our family appears to have been spared these problems.

The most dreaded of all afflictions, Cancer (my mother was unable to even say that word...she called it "Der Eilige Sache"...the sickness thing) was purely a surgical disease at the time and the survival was limited. Breast, bowel, stomach, uterus and later lung cancers were the principal primary sites and although breast cancer patients did reasonably well (at least for a while) some of the others had little or no hope. My mother's frequent and unhappy pronouncement, which typifies the then prevalent approach to the management of cancer of the abdomen was "the doctor opened her up and had to close"....that was the way she described what happened to her sister Becky (Milt and Bob Watzman's mother) and her sister-in-law Rachel (Dorothy and Esther's mother). She nursed them both at Bluff Street and possibly at Crombie Street until they died (before I was born, I think) and described the horrors of dressing changes, open wounds, etc.

Psychiatric diseases were known...these were early Freudian and Jungian days and people were testing out the new terminology ...neurosis, schizophrenia, depression, id, ego, narcissism, Oedipus complex,

47

obsessive-compulsive disorders, etc., etc. We had a number of people in the family with character disorders but the only one that I remember with overt disease was my cousin Bernard who I think was autistic and probably schizophrenic.

The physicians who entered our lives in those days were pretty good for the time, I think. I had a pediatrician who predicted that I would not do well, because I didn't speak until I was almost four and because he thought the fontanelles in my skull had closed prematurely. My mother didn't believe him and often spoke of him as a "naar" (fool). Bob Cohen, my cousin served as our family practitioner when he had an office on Liberty Avenue before the war. Doctor Lewin was one of my father's pinochle players and he occasionally took care of some of our ills. When I was operated on at Montefiore for my ruptured appendix, I think the surgeon was a Dr. Frankenstein who was probably the second best known...Tom Shube was far and away the most prominent Jewish surgeon. My mother received some injections for her varicose veins from him, I believe and was later operated upon by Sidney Kaufman. My father's allergist was a Dr. Criep, I think, but maybe not...in any event, he received shots forever it seems to me and they didn't help his hay fever very much.

I don't think I can end this chapter without a summation of our family epidemiologic picture. We can take the two sides separately and see how they fared. On the Mankin side, if one excludes Becky who died of cancer early in her life, vascular disease predominated. All of Hymie's brothers died before the age of 50 and all but one had coronary artery disease. Only Joe was excluded because his heavy smoking caused a lung cancer and he died of that before his coronaries gave out. Hypertension was present, I believe in three of them, Harry, Leonard and Jack but Hymie and his two sisters were spared which presumably extended their lives. All lived to be over 80 but all died eventually of coronary vascular disease (I admit that I am not sure about Goldy). Their progeny have also had some coronary artery disease, but not nearly so prevalent. Milton died of it at a young age and Arthur had multiple episodes, the first at about 55; I did well until I bypass when I was past 80 (as my mother would say "cananahourie"). Aside from cousin Sandy (Leonard's son) who had hypercholesterolemia, hypertension and angina), none of the rest that I know of had significant vascular disease (I have to say that I have little information about Henry Monsky or Bernard Mankin both of whom may be dead of causes not known to me).

On the Simon's side the picture is far more variable. I don't know what happened to Sam's twin or when it occurred so if he (or she) is excluded that leaves us with eight siblings in that generation. One had coronary artery disease associated with diabetes, one had cancer, and all but one of the rest died of cerebral vascular disease or Alzheimers mostly in their 80's or beyond while institutionalized (Mary set the record at 104 and Jennie was also very long-lived). Since Jennie was also diabetic that means we had 2/8 with diabetes, one with cancer and the remaining 5 with cerebral vascular disease. Several including Rosie and Mary had hip fractures.

In the second generation of Simons family if one excludes the three Mankin boys (they are included with the other side above) we have a cuzship of 19 members. Nine of these had or have long fairly healthy lives. Three (Davy Simons, Bob Lechtner and Bob Watzman) died of coronary or cerebrovascular artery disease (Bob Lechtner also had a lung cancer) relatively young. Several have had Alzheimer's or other cerebral problems. Four died young of malignancies including one of myeloma, one of breast, one of colon and one of bladder cancer. One, Marvin Lechtner died of unknown causes, possibly trauma.

If I can be allowed a comment regarding these data, I think it is fair to say that the health statistics for the first generation cuzship reflect the improvement in medical care in the country in general. There is little doubt that the cuzship members had a considerably increased longevity as compared with the immigrant group (except on the Simon side where such long survivors as Mary, Harry and Jenny skew the statistics for the older group); while the children of the cuzship group (now second generation) are likely to live even longer and have fewer disease states.

A Last Look at Crombie Street:

I was privileged to spend a large part of my life in Pittsburgh. In addition to being born and raised on Crombie Street, I went to Pitt undergraduate and Medical Schools and after a period time away (1953-1960) came back to the University to join Dr. Ferguson in the Orthopaedic Department at the Medical School. I left again in 1966 but have been back many times for all kinds of occasions, including Milton and Hymie's deaths, selling the house on Crombie Street, Mary's birthdays, illnesses, operations and funeral, trips to the Cemetery and family celebrations of one sort or another. Since those days on Crombie Street I have followed the life and times of Mary, Hymie, Milton, Cecille (Milton's wife), Arthur, Specialty Clothing Company, the cousins and in fact the nieces and nephews.

It is all changed now...nothing is the same. Crombie Street still exists but the houses are different and even the street (no more cobblestones) and sidewalk seem altered. The gardens and yards look different and seem to have had far less care. And Murray Avenue....it is different too. The attempt to gentrify Murray Avenue has only succeeded in making it look tawdry and has destroyed its Yiddish charm. The street car tracks have been dug up, the stores are different and the remarkable feelings about it that I had in the past are all gone.

Colfax school looks the same (Cua's is gone) but Allderdice has taken on a new and not really architecturally pleasing look....it seems to more closely resemble a prison now (that may not be far off from reality!). So all the things that are described above and the way I saw them will have to remain in my fading memory.... but happily are now down on these written pages. If you are a member of this family, then you too should retain this information and offer it to your children and grandchildren so that that can understand more about their roots and heritage....it is a proud one and they should know it.

CHAPTER 3: MEMORIES OF CROMBIE STREET...THE WAR YEARS

The years between 1936 to 1946 were monumental ones for the world, for Pittsburgh and particularly for me...living on Crombie Street during my adolescence. In 1936, I was 8 years old...and the depression was one year younger...Roosevelt was just completing his first term in office and his NRA (National Recovery Act) with all its components was just beginning to deal with the problems of unemployment and poverty. The WPA had started to put people back to work and jobs, initially created by the government had helped to rouse the sleeping industrial complex...which in turn began to increase both its manpower and productivity. The unions were beginning to fight for the rights of their employees and names like John L. Lewis of the UMW and Walter Reuther of the UAW appeared constantly in our newspapers and on the radio. Strikes and union contracts became the watchwords of the day. Consumer goods became less scarce and people began to buy. Prices were going up (a suit at Specialty Clothing Company now cost $17.00 instead of $14.00...but still with two pairs of pants!) and it seems that almost weekly we sat at the radio and heard

President Roosevelt begin his fireside chat with the words "My friends..." in a way so unique and distinctive, that I can shut my eyes and hear it now! His messages were ones of optimism and brought some hope of recovery from a terrible time.

I don't really exactly recall when I began to hear things about Europe and the mounting evidence that war was about to occur but it must have been around when I was 9 or 10. We noted some increase in concern in the papers with almost daily front page stories (one had to read the headlines on the front page before turning to the funnies) and particularly on the radio and the newsreels at the movies. Gabriel Heatter was our radio news analyst and he and some of the younger people who were just starting out (including the later-to-be-famous war correspondents Eric Severeid and Edward R. Murrow) told us of Hitler's rise to power; of the German brown-shirts, the Hitler Youth, the Gestapo and the SS; of giant crowds listening for hours to speeches by their dictators ...interrupting frequently by saluting and shouting "Sieg Heil"; of the inaction of the other European countries and the futile attempts on the part of Neville Chamberlain and Eduoard Deladier to slow the pace of German aggression; and ultimately the invasions of the Sudatenland, Czechoslovakia, Austria and Poland all in the name of first nationalism and then the quest for "Lebensraum". It was sort of unreal though, all of that, almost like a movie or a book and I guess lots of people agreed with that. There was a mood of isolationism in our government and our people, most of whom were still licking their depression wounds and were not terribly interested in things happening on another continent to people whose languages we couldn't understand. After a while, people tired of reading or hearing about Goebbels, Goehring, Himmler, Mussolini, Chamberlain (with the inevitable umbrella) and were more concerned with the economy, the dust bowl in Oklahoma (Steinbeck's famous novel, *The Grapes of Wrath* took place in the mid 30's), strikes, the floods (the famous Johnstown flood!)

and of course, baseball with Babe Ruth and Lou Gehrig dominating the national scene but in Pittsburgh we had our very own heroes, Pie Traynor and Gus Suhr.

I am not sure when I first heard about Nazi anti-Semitism and Hitler's attempt to destroy the German Jews but somehow it crept into our sensibilities and then became a glaring and blatant concern. I guess my first contact was related to the kids who began appearing in our classes in Colfax Elementary School. Miriam Kornitzer, Hans Jonas, Mimi Oppenheimer, Rolf Winter and others drifted into our lives. They were Jewish (but not really "Yiddish" ...there's a distinction), had accents, dressed a bit differently at first and were "outsiders" at least for a while. The boys didn't know how to play baseball and the girls didn't wear bobby sox. Some of them told us stories...kid's stories of things that happened that made some of us at least wonder about Europe and the Nazis. Then in Hebrew and Sunday schools we were told of atrocities against our people and Rabbi Rose's sermons during Saturday Services (I had begun studying for my Bar Mitzvah and hence had to attend every Saturday...Mr. Baradon's orders!) became increasingly strident in expressing concern for our people in Europe. We heard the words "Concentration Camp" (I have admit to not being able to guess as to the meaning of the word "concentration" in this context and I thought it had something to do with the demand that the Jews concentrate and give serious thought to their errant ways!), Kristallnacht (the night they broke all the windows in the Jewish shops and houses) and then gas chambers...an unspeakable horror which was described only in a whisper and which most people couldn't believe really occurred (some today still don't believe that it happened!).

I guess my mother was the most vehement in her hatred of the Germans and believed the worst about the Nazi's treatment of the Jews. Maybe my father and the rest of my uncles and aunts did too, but I don't think they were in Mary's league in ability to see the worst in people. Mary hated the Germans (also the Poles, the Lithuanians and the Russians...but the Germans, or as she called them..."The Fluken" were the worst of all) and I guess based on her European experiences as a child, she really believed that they were quite capable of rounding up the Jews and putting them in camps. I am not sure that she believed that the Jews were being killed, at least at first, but I think that by the time we went to war in 1941 she was convinced that Jews were dying by the thousands in Europe and I guess we all agreed with her. It was a bad time for Jewish people in Pittsburgh and all of the US...none of us wanted to believe it was happening, and when we did believe it we didn't know what to do about it. Our government wasn't really interested in listening to what sounded to us by then to be deafening cries of despair and death rattles of our people.

When Hitler's Panzer divisions crossed into the lowlands and France it was apparent that the world was really at war. The Dutch and Belgian suffering was bad and the French capitulation was pathetic (what ever happened to the Maginot line? One day it was there and the next day it was gone!). Britain entered the war and we all cheered...thinking that their fighting men and machines would end it in a short time. But the Nazi Wehrmacht was really a mighty force (much more so than the world appreciated up to that point in time) and so we read in the papers and heard on the radio or saw in the movie news bad stories about Dunkirk, mobilization for war, the bombing of Britain, blackouts, rationing and the inevitable deaths of so many young fighting men. It wasn't hard for the kids of the day to become very involved in the war. My friends, Leroy Weiner, Sonny Gottlieb, Alan Udell, Marvin Gusky, etc. and I were now approaching 13 and studying for our Bar Mitzvahs...but in our fantasy lives walking to or from the Beth Sholom we became Spitfire pilots, our planes roaring over the English Channel and downing Messerschmitts by the score; or patriots fighting with the Underground in France to liberate the French (usually beautiful young ladies of almost inevitably Jewish extraction) from the yoke of Nazi occupation.

When the United States began losing their neutrality by engaging in Lend-Lease (a Roosevelt and Hopkins way of justifying sending almost anything to England) they sent Liberty ships...freighters laden with first food and then munitions to our friends the British. We were their lifeline and I guess we all took their side... and even the isolationists and America Firsters came around. American flying hero Charles Lindberg still argued for a posture of neutrality and Senator Harold Ickes was with him, but most everyone else cheered the Brits when they won a skirmish and cried for them when bad things happened. We now openly hated the Germans and to a lesser extent the Italians and people with accents or German surnames began worrying about possible reprisals. Some of the Liberty ships were sunk by the Nazi U-boats and the east coast cities became concerned about attack from the sea. I guess Boston and New York and maybe Baltimore and Philadelphia had blackouts and test air raids and even in Pittsburgh, we had an air raid siren that was tested every week (Monday if I remember!).

None of us really thought that we would go to war....although it became apparent to anyone who read the newspapers or listened to the radio that we were really supporting the Allies in the period from late 1939 on. We were rocked by the battle of Britain, cheered at the always understated valor of the British and listened with tears in our eyes when Churchill described "their finest hour". The war began to intrude...defense plants began to work two and then three shifts; the government in 1941 passed the Selective Service Act (which we knew as the "draft") and General Hershey took the first number out of the bowl to call up the lucky recruit; phrases like 1A (fully draft eligible) and 4F (not eligible by reason of health) crept into our vocabulary; and we were told to buy defense bonds and all the kids bought stamps in school...pasted them in books and when the total come to $18.75 traded them in on a $25 bond (all called initially "defense" bonds and stamps but then became "war" bonds and stamps). More and more Americans volunteered in England or with the Canadians to fight in Europe and the war against Germany now became our fight... admittedly without the deprivations of war for our civilians or the maiming and deaths for the boys in the front lines.   Our first set of war movies started showing and were immensely popular and fanned the flames of our now very active adolescent fantasy lives.

Then came Sunday December 7th in the year 1941...it was midafternoon when the news of Pearl Harbor reached Pittsburgh and I (and almost everyone who lived through it) shall never forget how stunning the news was. I had just turned 13 (my Bar Mitzvah had occurred in October of 1941) and was playing basketball at the Irene Kaufmann Settlement on Centre Avenue in the Hill District.   We were in the middle of the game when someone came in and announced loudly that the Japanese had bombed Pearl Harbor and we were at war! President Roosevelt came on the radio and talked about the "day of infamy"...and we who had sort of watched and cheered the war from afar as interested spectators suddenly became major players and in what sounded to anyone who thought about it, a very bad game. We now had a war on two fronts...Europe and the Pacific and it didn't take long to realize that we were woefully unprepared for either. Our Pacific fleet had been badly damaged at Pearl Harbor and our troops although partly trained were really no match for the seasoned German Wehrmacht or the fanatical Japanese. Our air force was not really combat ready and our bases throughout the US and elsewhere were poorly organized and inadequately staffed for a war effort. The Government was stunned; the Military were in chaos; the people didn't know what was next and feared land or air attacks on our major cities ...and Pittsburgh shared in all of that...we just didn't really understand the meaning of war and what to expect....we were deeply troubled by all of that and particularly concerned that the newsreels showing destruction of cities, bombing of civilians and long lines of refugees going from place to place could now be about us instead of the Poles, Czechs or Chinese. It was terrifying in one sense but in another it represented a challenge...a chance to get into the game and play (but only to win...no one ever thought we could lose!) instead of watching from the sidelines.

Pittsburgh and the War:

In 1941 and 1942, Pittsburgh which had always been a large producer of steel became the world center for production of this crucial material...iron ore from the Mesabi range, coal from the coal mines in Pennsylvania, West Virginia and nearby Ohio came together in the blast furnaces and Bessemer converters of companies such as Jones and Laughlin, Bethlehem Steel and National Tube in the city itself and up and down the Monongahela valley to make the raw materials from which were fashioned the tools of war. Every plant worked three shifts and the skies were darkened by their output. It seemed like everyone in the county worked in the mills or in jobs that supported the people who worked there and there was a remarkable singlemindedness of purpose...make more steel to lick Hitler and the Nazis...to teach Tojo a lesson ...to build bombers and tanks that ultimately would triumph in North Africa, Italy, France, the islands of the South Pacific and south east Asia. Employment was not only full for the steel workers but because of the shortage of males as a result of the draft, women and part-time teenagers had jobs either in the mills themselves or in restaurants, food and department stores, theatres and even the city government. Everyone was working...it was a period of intense activity and the cheerfulness related to this productivity was felt throughout not just the city but all of Western Pennsylvania.

It wasn't all good though...there was the draft and all the young men who were called to Service some never to return. Red, white and blue banners appeared in windows on Crombie Street and all the other streets of Squirrel Hill (and everywhere) signifying that a member of the household was in the military service; and increasingly over the years more of these had gold stars indicating that the person had died. All the able bodied men were called up to the United States Army or enlisted in the Navy or Marine Corps and my brother Milton was one of the first on Crombie Street to go. Milt was called up at the same time as Fred Kelly who along with his brother, Gene Kelly ran a dancing school for the young ladies (and occasionally boys) of Pittsburgh. Milt and Fred and a lot of others were inducted into the Army in that first wave and after a period of basic training, because Milt was a college graduate with a background in science (my mother wanted Milton to be a doctor), he was stationed at Pine Bluff Arsenal in Arkansas, a chemical warfare base. No one ever really figured out why Milt went there or if he did anything while there, but one thing was true, he really hated it. His best times were when he came home on leave and met with his friends Lenny Hahn, Al Ainisman and Rube Snyderman to tell them stories of how miserable the Service was. Milton, always graceful and handsome was really a spectacular sight in uniform and a source of mixed feelings to the Mankins....pride (Pop and me) and deep foreboding and concern (Mary and Aunt Rosie). In addition to Milton, lots of the family went into the military: Bob and Milt Watzman, Davy and Eddie Simons, the two Korman boys from New York, Bob, Benny and Jack Lechtner from Erie and our cousin Bob Cohen the general practitioner was in for almost the entire war, and came out as a psychiatrist. Arthur was exempted probably because of his eyesight (he and I are both quite nearsighted) or maybe because he was in college at the time. He finished at Pitt in 1941 and went to graduate school at the University of Minnesota so had pretty much left the scene when I entered High School at the height of the war. I was 13 in 1941 and was 17 on VJ Day so really just missed. My cousins Sandy, Gerald, Morty, Sidney and Bernard I were all too young to see service although a number of us like Gerald, Sandy and I were drafted during the Korean campaign. None of the family were killed or wounded although several went overseas and saw combat. That was not true for some of my brothers' friends and even some people I knew in high school...it was sad when you heard about people dying in the war. It was high drama and heroic when it happened with appropriate background music in the movies but really just sort of tragic in real life when you realized that a guy you knew all those years died somewhere in a country he never even heard of before and was never going to come back.

Back home some of the things that happened were fun...some pretty scary...and some just silly. We had rationing and using ration books for meat, sugar and even shoes became a way of life. The real problem was gasoline rationing, especially for my father who in large measure made his living as a traveling salesman. There were all degrees of rationing for gasoline (A thru E) based on your need for an automobile and my father had a C rating, which was pretty good since his work depended on it. Lots of others were quite restricted in their travel. Food rationing was less of a problem to us...mostly because Mary was so frugal about what she cooked and really hated meat. So "Meatless Tuesday" was not a problem and as long as she could get some chicken or some delicious Lake Erie whitefish (neither rationed), we ate well. I am sure anyone who knew my mother could picture her doing her shopping on Murray Avenue and even when things were scarce, coming home with provisions ...she was hard to deny! I remember Milt coming home on leave and Mary spending all of family ration tickets for a two week period on a beautiful rib roast (Milt's favorite)...but she didn't do anything like that for us. I should also point out that anytime you have rationing like that you also can count on black market activity and Pittsburgh was no exception to that rule. There was a black market in all kind of stamps and even more so in buying the products without ration books. I don't think people made very much money on this kind of activity...it was just part of the antisocial response to any kind of law...to figure out a way to break it... and of course get away with it!

Another thing we had in Pittsburgh was blackouts....and I am not sure why we couldn't light our electric signs or use automobile lights late at night but apparently someone was concerned with bombing or whatever, so we did. We had air raid tests complete with sirens and everyone going to the basement. Air raid wardens wore their hats and arm bands and told us where to go. I don't know what we would have done if an enemy plane had actually appeared on the horizon but all of us were prepared to identify it. We took lessons in profile identification so we could tell a Messerschmitt from a Fokker from an American or British plane. We actually made models of these just to learn what a B17 looked like and how to distinguish it from its German counterpart. We even learned to identify Japanese Zeros and I guess that was the ultimate in silliness for Pittsburgh but it seemed like the right thing to do at the time.

The ladies volunteered their time at the high school for things like rolling bandages (did anyone ever use those thousands and thousands of rolled up strips of linen?) and of more purpose, entertaining our Servicemen at the local USO canteens by baking cookies, passing out donuts and even dancing with them. It was all right for ladies in their 20's but some of the girls in our high school classes at age 12-15 put on their snoods, too much makeup and wore silk stockings in order to "pass". I think most of that was innocent but we all watched the movies about the Stagedoor Canteen in New York and knew the words of the song about losing your heart at it...and it isn't hard to guess the way a bunch of teenage boys rewrote those words! Everyone was supposed to write to servicemen and letter writing to my brother became a weekly chore for me...it was actually kind of fun telling him the news of the week although he rarely wrote back. Some of the girls in our class adopted servicemen and wrote them long and passionate letters, sending them pictures with more makeup than they have used since and hoping that they would grow up before the guys came home. I wonder if anyone saved those letters and what a treasure they would be to read now....fifty years later!

Patriotism and loyalty to country became our watchwords; the President and our armed Services were uppermost in our minds and indeed in our hearts. We still did the Lord's prayer in school in the morning but along with it we saluted the flag and on every possible occasion sang the Star Spangled Banner....just imagine a bunch of teenage boys with voices cracking tackling that song!...but we did it with feeling and a stirring in our hearts. Most of the boys couldn't wait to grow up so that they too could join the military and I remember trying to learn to read eye charts without my glasses so that when the time came I could qualify as 1A! It was a time of unity for the American public, perhaps the last such in our history. We all worked together, black and white, bosses and workers, Jew and Gentile, Catholic and Protestant for the war effort. Anything that anyone did which in threatened our production of war materials or compromised our soldier's ability to fight the enemy was not only viewed with scorn but was roundly condemned by everyone...almost as one voice. It really was one voice and I guess the voice that we listened to most was Franklin Delano Roosevelt who told us what we needed in a way that mesmerized us and drove us to even greater heights of patriotism. It was a bad time for the world and for the people who were killed or tortured but it was a good feeling to be a part of the war effort in Pittsburgh in those years. I shall never forget them...and I think anyone who went through them will remember them as vividly as I do.

Taylor Allderdice High School:

I graduated from Colfax Elementary School in June of 1940 and in September, at the age of 12, I entered Taylor Allderdice High School to spend the next six years there in Junior and Senior High. As noted in the first chapter, Taylor Allderdice (named after a little known and scarcely remembered former President of the Board of Education of the City of Pittsburgh) was only two blocks from Crombie Street so it took me all of 5 minutes to get to school on any day and it was easy (and in fact knowing Mary, absolutely mandatory) to come home for lunch most days. I don't recall eating lunch in the lunch room very often although occasionally Mary would give me 35 cents to buy a meal in one of the lunch periods (the school was so big and the lunch room so small that there were three periods...early, middle and late, each a half hour in duration). I actually liked the meatballs and spaghetti (15 cents) and especially the mashed potatoes which came with a serving of thick grayish colored meat gravy (10 cents) and I still remember the rolls and butter (5 cents) which were quite tasty.

Allderdice was an unusual school by Pittsburgh standards, chiefly because it had a heterogeneous population of students. It was big...about 2000 students and in the war years each class consisted of about 300 students. Just about half of the students came from Squirrel Hill and the other half from Greenfield and Homewood. Squirrel Hill was (and still is) principally a white collar Jewish neighborhood with middle class people south of Forbes Street and upper middle class north of Forbes (an important social dividing line which figured prominently in our lives as we entered the dating age!). Greenfield and Homewood were for the most part heavily Catholic and principally working class people, many of them blue collar. Most of the families in Squirrel Hill hoped and indeed expected their children to aspire to a college education and professional careers; most of those from Greenfield had far less concern for education or aspirations for their children. Needless to say the kids from Squirrel Hill were more than just competitive over grades...they were at times frantic...those from Greenfield for the most part didn't care very much. There were obviously exceptions. Not everyone in Squirrel Hill was a scholar and there were also many Gentile families living both north and south of Forbes. Conversely, some of our most talented students came from Greenfield. There was also the intermediary zone...the other side of Murray Avenue past Forward. The kids who lived there were close to the Greenfield side and had a more difficult time with cultural relations than those who lived on Darlington (near the Manor theatre) for instance or even more so those that lived on Inverness or Bennington, north of Forbes. I should point out that a lot of the kids from North of Forbes attended private schools...Shadyside Academy for the boys and Winchester or the Ellis School for the girls, so the rest of us only met them at social events.

Cultural relations between the two groups of students were sometimes strained. The words "cultural relations" is perhaps a polite euphemism for some pretty blatant anti-Semitism which was acted out by the boys in the form of fights and other hostile acts. I learned about this shortly after entering Junior High when I was beaten by a group of kids in the Men's room...not badly...I had a few outwardly evident bruises ...but the real ones were inside chiefly because I very quickly realized two things: first, that I was not invincible but in fact, quite vulnerable; and second, that I could be hated for something I had no control over. I learned an important lesson very early...not everyone is going to love you! For the most part there was a little of this going on all the time but it was not really very overt or blatant nor did it significantly interfere with education or social events. In my whole time there we had only one real skirmish that we called a "race riot" ...the kids from Greenfield came over to Squirrel Hill in gangs looking for people to attack...it didn't last very long and no one was hurt. I guess what I found most unpleasant about it was the undercurrent of hostility. There were some people from the other side who I thought were good folks and with whom I wanted to be friendly but felt constrained not to approach them and I am sure it was the same for some of them.

In Junior High, we were assigned to home rooms where we met every morning, pledged allegiance to the flag, said the Lord's prayer, and then went out to our various classes going from one to another but back to the home room for a study period, usually right after lunch. We also had assembly periods when the entire class and sometimes large groups of students met in the auditorium to hear presentations, attend pep rallies and see the class play or listen to musical performances. The Choral Group under Miss Steiner were regular performers as were Orchestra A under Laura Ziegler. We had some virtuosos who performed as well. One of the most memorable of these performances was that of Marshall Levy and Nancy Freedman playing a piano duet (two pianos) version of "Tea for Two" with a lot of improvisation ...what talent some of the kids had! The motto over the stage in the Auditorium was important..."Know Something; Do Something; Be Something" ...it's hard to forget that message.

Some of the more memorable teachers for me included Miss Quatrocchi who taught civics and social studies, Mr. Wagner, math, Miss Simpson, a stern and forbidding Latin teacher, Miss Brennan a really outstanding teacher of German, and Miss Bergman (who subsequently became my home room teacher in senior high school) who taught Spanish and was sort of dippy. Then there were the coaches. Ernie Schlesinger was the football coach, John Irvin was responsible for track and field and the swim team and "Puss" Irwin coached the basketball team. The Principal was John D. McClymonds who joined us soon after I entered senior high school. He was famous in my mind for his opening comments at each graduation ceremony (annually at first but after a while during the war when classes were accelerated, every six months). The words were "Classes come and classes go and after a while they all seem to merge into one..." Then he would add a statement how this class was different! Being involved in education and graduating resident classes every six months for the past thirty years has heightened my appreciation for Mr. McClymonds observation and remarks and oddly enough I find myself using them quite frequently (like every six months or so!).

The most memorable of our teachers for most of us was Lon H. Colborn, the chemistry teacher. Mr. Colborn taught chemistry to anyone who wanted to learn...but he also had a special qualitative and quantitative analysis class...by invitation only...which met twice (or was it three times?) a week during the entire lunch period (1.5 hours). It was a special time for us in that class, partly because of the excitement of the subject material ("qual" and "quant" were just starting to become a standard technology then and required a lot of sometimes fascinating detective work) and the other students (surely Allderdice's elite, at least in terms of intelligence); but mostly because of Mr. Colborn himself. As I look back on my educational life, he stands out as most influential in guiding me into a world of productive science....and everyone who came in contact with him (and there were lots of us) felt the same way. The mysterious part is no one was ever sure how he exerted his influence on his charges and why so many of them achieved the way they did...and they really did achieve. He once published his private memoirs and it was hard to believe, if you hadn't been there, the numbers of deans, college professors, scientists, physicians and prominent business people...all united by that year in

Colborn's Qual and Quant class! It is true that he carefully chose the substrate and in fact was an "intellectualist" if such a word exists...but it was more than that. I guess he taught us to ask questions, doubt the answers and, where there were no easy answers, to seek them out. That's a formula I have tried to imbue in my students but I am afraid far less successfully than Lon Colborn. I think we all owe him a lot...certainly I do.

Taylor Allderdice was a good school and at least at the time the academic record was really quite exceptional. There was ample opportunity to learn and the teachers for the most part were interested in teaching their students. They weren't always good at teaching but they all tried hard and most often succeeded. We had clubs...science club, chess club, Spanish club, math club, geography club, etc. all run by the teachers and enthusiastically attended by them and the students. Our teachers tutored at times and really worked to get everyone through. But I think the difference between our student body and subsequent ones is that we really read...read for school, read for learning, read for entertainment or just read to read. We had a good library at Allderdice and it was really well used, but most of us had as our fondest possession our Carnegie Library card and waited eagerly for Saturday or after school or an off school day to go there, browse amongst the stacks and take out as many books as we could carry. I don't think there was anyone in our entire school that couldn't read...and among my friends from Squirrel Hill, most of us read with a passion and a desire that I don't think has ever been equaled in my experience since.

Bar Mitzvah...the Great Event:

If you are a Jewish male, there are some ceremonies that happen to you that are for the most part out of your control. The first of these is the "Bris" the ritual circumcision which occurs usually at under 1 week of age. It is a remarkably ceremonial event with a special person to hold you (the Bible said it should be your father...but even for the old-time Jewish people that was a bit much so there was a "Sondek", a designated father substitute!), another special person to make the incision in your foreskin (the "Mohel") and a whole bunch of relatives and friends to watch, congratulate the mother (who is in another room!) and the father (who usually faints!) and then eat cake and have a little wine in honor of the occasion. If you are the first born male in your family you have another party in your honor, also in the first week or so of life, this one a lot less painful...no cutting, just a lot of Hebrew prayers. That's called the "Pidyen ha Ben". The third ceremony is the Bar Mitzvah...the coming of age...the event at age 13 that signifies in the eyes of the community and the Lord, that you are now a "man" and can enter all the prayer rituals and participate as an adult when the prayer system requires 10 men (a "Minyan") to start a Service. Speaking as a Jewish male who underwent two of the three rituals (I was the third born so was spared the Pidyen ha Ben) I have to express my admiration for Yiddish timing....just imagine if the Bar Mitzvah and the Bris were reversed in time and the circumcision occurred at age 13!

So on to the Bar Mitzvah...every Jewish boy's nightmare! The preparation began when I was about 8 and started Hebrew School. We went every afternoon five days a week, except in the winter when Erev Shabas (the Sabbath eve which began at sundown), came too early in the day for school to continue. Shortly thereafter, my Mother and Aunt Rosie began telling me about the great Bar Mitzvahs in the family and how proud they were going to be when I did mine. I was too young to remember Milt's (he was 12 years older than me and hence I would have been 1 year of age) but I remember Arthur's. The picture is a bit vague but I do remember that he was so short at the time that he had to stand on a box to give his speech! The actual preparation began when I had to start attending Saturday Services to watch the others and was formally introduced to our teacher, Mr. Baradon.... indeed a fearsome and formidable individual. He had the task of shaping, instructing and somehow turning out for public display, one Bar Mitzvah "Bocher" (young lad) a week...and if my level of enthusiasm was representative, not an easy task at all!

First we had to learn to read Hebrew...difficult at best. The words go from right to left (rather than the English left to right); the consonants are characters which don't look a bit like English...but have sounds like ours with some missing and some added; and the vowels are subscript characters added onto the consonants. The printed words are hard to read...the script is next to impossible without a lot of practice. Furthermore the modern Hebrew writing world plays a trick on you because just when you think you are really getting good at reading Hebrew or Yiddish (a middle European polyglot language which originally had no alphabet but adopted the Hebrew characters....but with almost completely different sounds and meanings to the words!), they take away the vowels and then it really gets tough! Reading is of course one thing...understanding is another and after a year or two of Hebrew school most of us could read the language pretty passably...but very few of us knew what we were reading. Understanding the words we said was not a requirement of the Bar Mitzvah at least at the Beth Sholom. At the time in the 1930's most people thought of Hebrew as a dead language like Latin and unless one wished to become a Rabbi or a Cantor, there didn't seem to be much advantage to learning it (as opposed to Spanish or German, for instance both of which we thought would be very useful in our future lives). In a way that was too bad because it robbed us of an opportunity to speak another language which over the intervening years has become an important one in the world and the principal way of communicating with a lot of our kin.

After we had learned our Hebrew well enough to first sound out the characters and then apply some word recognition and then develop an appropriate accent (some of the sounds are little difficult for the western tongue!), we had to learn some special things in preparation for the event. How to "lay Tefillin"...put on the phylacteries ...an ancient ritual designed to renew your faith by offering a solitary prayer to God each morning. Next we turned to learning the Bible reading and the explanatory passage that we were responsible for on our Bar Mitzvah Sabbath. The first, the Bible reading is a brief passage from the sacred scrolls (the Torah) that is assigned to our specific Saturday, which is supposed to be sung in traditional melody by the Bar Mitzvah boy. Because of the difficulty of reading it from the Torah... (there are no vowels and the characters are slightly different) and also the problems of interpreting the marks which signal alterations in the pitch of one's voice during the chant, frequently the celebrant himself does not do this but needs the services of a "specialist" ...a reader of the Torah (it is an honor if his father does it...and an even greater joy to the family if the Bar Mitzvah Bocher does it himself!). But the interpretation which is really an expansion of the tract in the Torah (known as the "Haftorah") is all for the Bar Mitzvah boy. He has to stand on the pulpit in his new Bar Mitzvah suit...all alone to deliver a passage which to him seems eternal in duration which must be sung accurately and sung well. Everyone in the Synagogue listens carefully, particularly the parents (praying that they won't be disgraced), the old timers in their long Talassim (prayer shawls) and the quaking pre-Bar Mitzvah Bochorim waiting for their turns in the next few weeks! It was a test not only of the ability to perform in that setting but of the stability of one's voice which in about 50% of us would start out as tenor and change suddenly during the chant to either squeaking boy soprano or croaking basso profundo!

Then comes the final test...the speech. The Bar Mitzvah boy now must address the audience in English and give a speech, politely expressing gratitude to one's parents, the Rabbi, Mr. Baradon, the congregation and the entire Jewish community for allowing him to join them as a "man". This should be drawn out as long as possible to reduce the need for the next section, which consists of an attempt to put the section of the Torah read that day into prospective with current events, such as the World Series, the National Recovery Act, the Spanish Civil war, etc. This usually doesn't work but one can end strongly by declaring your manhood ...(I think the words I said were "Today I take my place in Jewish society as a man and I pledge that I shall remain dedicated to Jewish principles"...it's a wonder some bolts of lightning don't come out of the ceiling every Shabas!). Winding that speech up left only one ordeal...the Rabbi's remarks.... directed at the entire congregation, but delivered standing face to face with the Bar Mitzvah Bocher and only a few feet away. I and all my colleagues prayed that his breath wouldn't be too bad and that there would be no snickers from the other Bochorim in the first row...it just wouldn't do to start laughing hysterically at that point in time. Then...wonder of wonders...it's over...you've done it...you have completed the Bar Mitzvah ceremony and it is time for the parties. First the party in the Sisterhood Hall which takes place immediately after the closing benediction. The adults come to taste the wine and eat some strudel (Mary baked for weeks for this occasion!) while the children (excuse me...I was just designated a man!) run about and play...interrupted only by a series of relatives who press envelopes containing money gifts into your hand or give you a gift wrapped box (small is a fountain pen...large is a sweater!). Finally on Saturday night, there was the evening party for the family, in my case held on Crombie Street. After I received all the handshakes from my uncles (and a few more gifts!) and kisses from my aunts, I spent the evening as I usually did on such occasions talking to my cousins Bernard and

Sidney or teasing my cousins Joanne and Lucille. As I recall the event, it was a happy time for me...as I think it is for every Bar Mitzvah boy. I am sure there are words for the way I felt like the "rites of passage" or some such, but it is for every Jewish child, an exceptional event ...a milestone...and maybe it really is a turning point...a time of change in life ...of putting away the more childish things and turning to the serious business of being a "man".

Neighbors, Friends and Heroes:

In the late 30's the people in the Crombie Street neighborhood began to change. Our next door neighbors the Kopelmans moved out and took my "first-best-friend" Myron away. I remember saying goodbye and feeling sad. Jerry and Dorothy Solomon moved in...he was a lawyer...she was a good hearted but not very bright lady who my mother loved to mimic. They had two daughters, Rita two years older than me and Phyllis two years younger. I liked both of them...Rita was sort of serious and shy... she was smart in school. Phyllis was less smart than her sister and it seemed to me, a little crazy...in retrospect I think she had petit mal seizures for at least a while...when we got older she was a little wild. We played together some of the time but with Selma Rogal still living in the next house up the street, the combination of that many girls and all that girl-talk was too much for me. I on the other hand was increasingly concerned with sports, particularly basketball and softball and other more "manly" things, and so concentrated my street social activities on my male neighbors. My new "best-friend" Leroy Weiner moved in across the street and almost at the same time Sonny Gottlieb moved in two doors away from him on Tilbury Street. Leroy and I were the same age but Sonny was a year younger. He went to the Poale Zedek Synagogue (the Orthodox Shul at the corner of Nicholson and Shady), was more religious than Leroy and me and wore a yarmulke (skull-cap). About half way up Crombie Street was Herbie Limsi, two years younger and sort of a flake but fun; and at the top of the street near Beechwood Boulevard were the Coffey twins about two years older than me, from a blue collar background and very good athletes. Most of my activities with this group of neighbors (especially Leroy and Sonny) occurred during the summer times when we had some time and although we saw each other in the winter, especially for sled riding (I remember when Arthur persuaded my mother to get us a sled...a Flexible Flyer!) it clearly was a much busier time.

Fall, winter and spring days were pretty full...school 'til 3:05 (it's funny how I remember the exact time when the Taylor Allderdice final bell rang...what a moment of joy that was on many days!), Hebrew school, Saturday Services and even Sunday School. Between those activities, working at Specialty Clothing Company during the busy seasons, homework and trips to the library, there wasn't a lot of time left over for socializing with friends on Crombie Street during the school months. But the three months of summer...now that was great fun and oh, how we relished every moment of it. No school, no Hebrew School, no Sunday school, no work at Specialty (the slack season!). We knew every inch of Frick Park (at the top of Crombie Street), went on long walks to Schenley or even Highland Park, joyfully went to the movies on Saturday afternoon (poor Sonny Gottlieb couldn't go because of Shabas), played softball and basketball at Colfax field, learned how to ride a bicycle (actually my brother Arthur taught me that!), went to the library together and read the funnies on Sunday morning in each other's houses.

I don't think my Crombie Street friends ever all got together at the same time and it seemed to me that my relationships were staged in time. We went through phases of "togetherness"...so that for a few summers Leroy, Sonny and I were inseparable; and then it was Herbie Limsi and Ernie Barash who moved in next door to Selma Rogal; and then the Coffey twins and some of their friends, etc.

I remember one summer when I was about 9 or 10, my Mother and Father decided that I ought to go to summer camp for two weeks and they chose Camp Kadimah, a Jewish camp not far from Pittsburgh run by a man named Solomon Osheroff. I don't think I cried when I went away...unlike a lot of the other kids who were homesick...and I remember not liking the meals very much but enjoying the outdoor activities and hoping that I could grow up to be a Counsellor someday. I remember having to write a post card home every few days (Mr. Osheroff insisted on that...it was the way of being sure that the parents would think well of his camp!). This is also where I first learned camp songs like "Pufferbelly" and "Someone's In The Kitchen With Dinah". I met a few new people there including Jackie Breskow who first initiated me conversationally at least into some of the more lurid aspects of sexuality. He talked about girls and their parts incessantly and although I had some knowledge prior to that (mostly out of books) Jack and some of his friends and I had some late night conversations (after our counsellor, Jerry Hydowitz, (a hero and later to become an internist colleague in Pittsburgh) had left us for the night) which clarified (or so I thought) some of my confusions about sex and the acts of love (or should I say lust!). I came back from Kadimah with a sunburn, lot of dirty laundry and some very dirty thoughts.

School friends were different. I saw more of them but it wasn't as close as it was with the neighborhood kids....we shared views and events but not as many secrets. Many of the school friends appeared in my life every day either in my home room or in classes and we ate lunch together, stood outside at the wall on Tilbury Street in a group or just hung around. I think in general either I liked everyone or these were a nice group of people...because it is hard to remember any real villains amongst my group. Aside from my street friends the first group that I grew close too were my Bar Mitzvah Club members...those who were Bar Mitzvah at the Beth Sholom in the same year as I was. There were in this group some very bright and capable people in many ways disparate in objectives and lifestyles (and as it turned out, subsequent careers) who still, because of the ordeal of the Bar Mitzvah, clung tightly together like passengers on a small boat in a storm. Melvin Feldman, Murray Love, Melvin Passekoff, Morris Tufshinsky, Marvin Gusky, Lloyd Whitman, Earl Latterman and a lot of others who went to Hebrew School together, were schooled not-so-patiently by Mr. Baradon and met as I recall every Sunday morning to learn the rituals, have a breakfast provided by the mothers (including Mary) and exchange greetings and stories about sports events and school happenings...and in a hushed whisper, always a breath away from a giggle, talk about girls (never in those days did we talk to girls...just talked about them!). Once the Bar Mitzvah was over the group drifted apart to start their adult lives but still when we chance to meet today, we smile affectionately at one another, perhaps remembering the shared experience of old days at the Beth Sholom.

The friends I made in school were people with whom for the most part I shared a common view of things and had concordant objectives and goals. The people I chose to be with (or perhaps since at the time I wasn't very outgoing, chose me) would by today's standards be known as "nerds". We were bright...the "intelligentsia"...the people who read widely, knew the answers in class, got A's on our tests, always did our homework, joined the science or the chess club, were on none of the athletic teams and later proved to be some of Lon Colborn's super-achievers. Melvin Passekoff, Sheldon Edelstein, Howard Corey, Herbie Labbie....I liked being with them...they were very stimulating and exciting in an intellectual way, but still at time I longed for and spent good times with my Crombie Street friends and Colfax School softball and Irene Kaufman Center basketball players...and others who challenged me less but with whom I was sometimes better able to communicate.

Girl friends were really just that...girls who were friends. I was friendly with my neighbors Selma Rogal, Rita and Phyllis Solomon and a few other young ladies, such as Hermoine Rubin (Leroy's cousin...one of my first crushes), my cousin Lois Skirboll who moved to the corner of Tilbury and Shady, Bernice Danovitz from Nicholson Street and sweet Sondra Silverman (very bright and warm and caring) who lived down the street from us on Tilbury. We shared things but didn't "date" or even talk about it...we were just class mates, homework sharers, occasional movie goers (always in a group) and friends. I remember being a little stunned when I saw some of my "girl friends" at Beth Sholom on Rosh Hashanah wearing their new dress-up clothes and I suddenly realized that they were almost women and subtly perhaps our relationships changed.

Somewhere around the 10th grade, I found myself involved with a special category of friends...my AZA buddies. AZA stands for American Zionist Association and we and our female counterparts, the BBG (Bnai Brith Girls) were really not devoted to Israel or interested in Aliyah or life on the Kibbutz. It was an opportunity for Jewish boys and girls to get together in an organization, hold dances and most of all play softball and especially basketball (I was crazy about that game...despite being only 5 feet 8 inches tall and not very good). We played everywhere...at Taylor Allderdice in an evening league, the Irene Kaufmann Settlement, the "Y" (Young Mens and Womens Hebrew Association in Oakland) and in tournaments in far off places like Altoona, Canonsburg, Elwood City, Beaver Falls, etc. against similar AZA groups from those places. My AZA friends included my second cousin Stanley Skirboll (a really nice person...unlike some of my relatives, we had a lot in common), Jerry Simon (our tall man on the team, all of 6 feet 1 inch), Lennie Schaffel (the lover...he had a long standing torrid relationship with Roz Robbins), Milt Hirsh (a little older and had a desperately needed car!), Bernie Naimark and a lot of others. We weren't very good at basketball or softball but we had a lot of fun in going through the phase of what now is probably termed male bonding, I suppose. We also became seriously interested in the opposite sex and had some tentative sexual adventures (rather tame, I am afraid by today's standards!) which became the subject of endless discussion. It was the right time for that I guess.

To say the least and to use an arcane phrase of yesterday, during the six years at Allderdice, I could not be considered a "social lion". I was a little shy, introspective, short and (yes, I admit it) fat and despite my father being in the clothing business didn't have a lot of clothes to wear...and frankly didn't care much about clothes. There were a number of people at Allderdice who had all the trappings of social awareness and success and I watched and in truth, envied them. In my mind they fell into two groups: north of Forbes people (I could call that group "genetic" in a sense that their parents were polished people with wealth and the same graces); and the "young-men-in-the-know" coterie (more "acquired" since many of their parents were immigrants like our family). Marcus Aaron, Martin Hamburger, Henry Grinsfelder and Carl Adelsheim were in the former class...they dressed in Brooks Brothers clothes, didn't speak Yiddish (and didn't speak to anyone who spoke Yiddish) went to Rodef Sholom Temple and had the social graces that one associates with country club kind of wealth. I was sure they wore a coat and tie for dinners at home. The other group typified by Hank Neaman, Herbie Arnold, Jerry Prince and Alfie Rosen had the kind of physical and social ease and grace I aspired to...they dressed well in the mode of the day, were athletic, physically impressive and laughed a lot and loudly. They all had reindeer sweaters (I didn't!), had worn tuxedos at one time or another, smoked (wow!) and could jitterbug (I had none of those attributes when I entered the 10th grade). I looked at those two groups of people with some envy...at times I designated them as "heroes" but not always since they had some glaring faults; but I guess I admired their social ease, which seemed to come so naturally to them and was seemingly so difficult for me.

I had some true heroes then too...they were people who were very popular at school principally because they were accomplished or remarkably talented. David Jandorf (a really great trumpet player), George Roth (a magnificent violinist from Orchestra A), Hank Neaman (a football player and really graceful person...he did everything well), Jerry Kramer (a fellow oboe player in the orchestra who seemed to know everything and everyone), Byron Yanks (later went to Julliard, changed his name to Janus and became an internationally known pianist), Irwin Schaefer (basketball player, bright...later a medical school classmate) and Nancy Freedman (a piano player and singer...one of my first from-a-distance crushes).

It is hard for me now to sort out how many of those friendships were really true friendships (and how do you define that anyway?) and how many were just knowing someone. At the time they were important to me and my image of myself and I guess having a lot of friends was important to all of us. As we grew older and drifted off to college, high school friends played less and less of a role in my life and I lost track of many or really most of these people. Now almost seventy years later, I mostly read about them when they die or something happens to them and then remarkably a memory springs into my mind; but the image I see is always as they were ...young, graceful and full of promise...not as I discover they really are when I meet them at reunions or by chance. I don't like seeing them as they are now...it profanes an important set of memories...and I really don't like thinking about the ones, like Leroy Weiner or Hank Neaman or Murray Love or Sonie Silverman who have died....I would rather remember them the way they were during Allderdice days.

Work and Play:

The work ethic was something that I came by honestly...my mother was the hardest working woman I have ever met. My father worked hard at Specialty Clothing Company but took some time out for baseball games, trips to visit relatives, vacations (at least during his hayfever season) and every Saturday night when he played Pinochle with his cronies. Not Mary...she never really relaxed ...and in fact that became worse with age! I started to work when I was very young and have never stopped and I think it is all because of her!

My first "job" consisted of going to the store on Sunday and making boxes (putting together cardboard suit boxes for the lucky customers) but that was only during the busy season. Sometime around the time when I entered Junior High School I started delivering papers for Frank Marcosky... he was the local Fagin who came around in his car full of newspapers and passed them out to a bunch of us kids who delivered the Pittsburgh Press on routes (for some reason roads like Route 19 were pronounced as "rootes" but when we talked about the streets where we delivered papers, we called those "rowtes"...I never knew why!). I think my first paper route paid about one-half a cent a paper (but the paper only cost 6 cents delivered!). When the war started it was hard to get delivery people so I graduated to a Post Gazette morning route. I got up each morning at 4:30 AM and actually delivered about 100 papers all to homes north of Forbes (and now received 1-2 cents a paper!). That route was an especially good one because of the spectacular tips at Christmas time. I enjoyed the solitude and the quiet of the really elegant north of

Forbes streets during those morning deliveries...and even more enjoyed stopping in Herman's Bakery on my way home at 6:15 right after they opened and buying some sweet rolls while they were still warm. I would come home, have a bath, have my sweet roll and coffee (my mother let me have one cup of coffee in the morning) and then went off to school. I don't know why I wasn't more fatigued during the day but somehow it didn't affect me much and I never went to bed before 10:00 PM.

A little later, I started working at the Nixon Theatre (our only legitimate theatre in Pittsburgh at the time) as an usher and really enjoyed that. I must have seen the Student Prince 20 times!
We did see some good shows though and I guess I got to really like stage performances in that setting. I also took part time jobs as a soda jerk at the Manor Pharmacy, sorting mail at the Post Office over Christmas, as an usher at Syria Mosque and as a busboy at the Pittsburgh Athletic Club (talk about seeing how the other three percent lived!); but my two continuous "real" jobs were at Polonsky's Hebrew National Delicatessen where I cut meat, waited on customers, made sandwiches, etc.; and of course at the Store...good old Specialty Clothing Company where I was now considered to be qualified to do everything from sweeping the floors to waiting on trade. Everywhere I worked I worked hard and got paid which gave me a little financial freedom. I bought a typewriter that I needed and some special things like a new bicycle (I had been riding Arthur's all these years) and a new first baseman's mitt. I also met a lot of people whom I otherwise wouldn't have met and made a few special friends; and I also learned some things about business and aspects of that way of life that I was otherwise sheltered from. Had I to do it all over, I might not have done so much but at the time, there was too much Mary in me to pass it up!

If Mary made me work hard, then the half of my gene structure that come from my Father said "hey kid, play a little too" and I did...at least I tried. It was wartime in Pittsburgh...school, Hebrew School, Sunday School, homework, paper routes, work activities all made for a busy life...but there had to be more. There were things to do that were called "fun"...and they included going to Kennywood Park...the amusement park beyond Homewood. There were two roller coasters, one scarier than the next, a Merry-Go-Round, the Old Mill, a Ferris wheel and all the other things one did...and that was fun. Taylor Allderdice held a school picnic annually at Kennywood with reduced rates for all the rides and everyone enjoyed that day. Mary went along for the first few and then decided I could go on my own...but I still had to take along a bag lunch....she didn't want me buying hot dogs and things that weren't good for me (or weren't Kosher....although she gave up on trying to save my soul from that particular devil somewhere around the 8th grade!).

Major league baseball was one of my favorite activities during the season and we could usually get really cheap seats in the bleachers (I remember them as costing 75 cents!); and then depending on the Pirate fortunes for that year, drift over to sit in unoccupied reserved or even box seats. It's funny to remember it that way, but we started going to baseball games before night games were possible and Forbes Field had no lights until after the war. So to go to a game during the school year either required that we "play hooky" (I wonder where that phrase came from? ...what is a "hooky"?) or go on weekends. But there was always the summer time and for a dollar (75 cents to get in, 15 cents for the hotdog and 10 cents for two cokes!) it was a great way to spend the day. There is something really exciting about the umpire standing up there and shouting "play ball!"...it still stirs me.

As to athletic activities I didn't like football very much but really loved basketball and softball. I played those as often as I could and wherever I could. I wasn't terribly good at either but enjoyed the scene and rapid pace of basketball and the intellectual aspect and remarkable grace of softball. But amazingly as I look back on it, kids like me in Squirrel Hill at the time really had a limited opportunity to become involved in sports activity. I never played golf as a child or adolescent nor have I ever made a serious try at playing tennis, handball or squash. Hockey was not a game played very often in Pittsburgh and despite the cold winters few of us ever became very accomplished on ice skates. I didn't ski then and in fact never have. I did learn how to roller skate and I actually did that pretty well and I and some of my friends played hockey on roller skates on Nicholson Street (it's the only one of our streets that was level and had little traffic!).

Music was another part of our lives that added an important dimension. My mother loved the violin (don't all Jewish mothers?) and bought one for Milton and tried to get him to play ...and failed...skipped Arthur (how come he was so lucky?)... and tried me....and failed again! Alas poor Mary was destined to never have a violinist in the family. For reasons not clear to me somehow, somebody at Taylor Allderdice decided I ought to play the oboe. I had no particular reason to do that and in fact never owned an oboe...I used one owned by the school. I took lessons first at school and subsequently on Saturday mornings at Carnegie Tech and got to be pretty good at it. I became second oboe in Orchestra A (Jerry Kramer was first oboe and played rings around me!), played alto saxophone (same keyboard) in the marching band and because of the war and the scarcity of oboe players, I appeared intermittently with all kinds of musical groups...theatre orchestras, woodwind quintets and little symphony orchestras (never the Pittsburgh Symphony or anything big-league...I wasn't that good!). Some of my friends played in jazz combos and dance orchestras. Marshall Levy became Buddy Marshall and played the piano with his own orchestra...made up of Allderdice people...Leroy Supowitz, Henry Hile, Sterling Yates and of course Nancy Freedman (who later became Nancy Reed when she went on to sing with Stan Kenton's band).

The music of the day was special to all of us...some of it was patriotic but some was jazz; and most of the ballads were soppingly romantic. It seems to me that every one of us learned every word of those songs...and in many cases I can still remember them clearly. Just singing the first lines sometimes brings back memories of people and places. "Seems to me we stood and talked like this before"..."Gonna take a sentimental journey"..."Missed the Saturday dance"..."'Til then, my darling please wait for me"..."My mama done told me"..."They tried to tell us we're too young" ..."Pardon me boy, is that the Chattanooga choo choo"..."Straighten up and fly right"..."Don't sit under the apple tree"....They all bring back images and scenes.

What did we do during the daylight hours, particularly in the summertime? There were the parks...Pittsburgh was blessed with three major parks: Highland Park with a zoo that at the time matched any in the country; Schenley Park which had a swimming pool and a track for running, a golf course and a fantastic Westinghouse Memorial fish pond; and Frick Park, near Crombie Street which had a lot of hills and a really extraordinary old golf course and the ruins of a clubhouse that were fun to explore. At the end of Schenley Park was the Carnegie Museum (dinosaur bones and lots of exhibits), Carnegie Library (I lived for my days in the library and what a wonderful day it was when I traded my child's card for an adult one!) and the Carnegie Music Hall...a beautiful place but vastly underutilized at least in those days.

Evenings at leisure consisted of movies (by this time we now had an "art theatre" in Squirrel Hill...the Beacon at

Beacon Street and Murray Avenue); slow dancing in the dim light with girls (see below) at Savers on Route 51 (juke boxes, dancing, cokes, sundaes, no liquor); and eating out at the Villa d'Este and Highland House in East Liberty, Jack Canter's in Oakland and Poli's, Joseph's Steak House and the Chinese restaurant in Squirrel Hill (all were among my favorites). It was in the Chinese restaurant that I first ate shrimp....I was sure that a bolt of lightning sent by Mary would come out of the ceiling for this deliberate act of breaking Kosher! I waited first for the punishment...and then for the guilt and contrition....but instead I just enjoyed it! There was a bowling alley on Murray Avenue where we could bowl with duckpins (25 cents a line...and you didn't have to wear special shoes) and drug stores to loiter in front of...the Beacon Pharmacy at Beacon and Murray, Phillips Pharmacy at Phillips and Murray and Rosen's Drugs at the corner of Shady and Forbes ....we might have a soda or glass of coke but mostly we just "hung out"....waiting for someone or something...I don't think I ever found out who or what and after a while I stopped doing it.

And then there were the parties...birthday parties, Bar Mitzvah parties, weddings, family celebrations of heaven's knows what and school dances (boys on one side and girls on the other looking at each other...a few couples out on the floor jitterbugging...more slow dancing...it was the only chance some of us had to dance with a Gentile girl from Greenfield!). We also had party-parties...no particular reason for them...just a Saturday night party at someone's house...wear a tie....bring a date or come stag....a little drinking...some necking if the host's parents weren't home or were asleep. These occurred with increasing regularity in my last few years at Allderdice and it seemed to me that they were our principal source of social interchange....and where we learned the rules of the "boy-girl game" (see below).

Just a word about addictive materials and substance abuse (new words... we didn't use them then)....a lot of the kids in our class started to smoke when it became fashionable around the age of 16 or so (some earlier...and some like me abstained). We didn't drink very much during high school and aside from a few beers at parties, I don't know any of our crowd who really got drunk...even on a dare. We didn't know anything about marijuana...although it must have been available... and uppers, downers, PCP, Quaaludes, cocaine, heroin and crack never appeared in our lives and most of us never even heard the words or could identify what they meant. It really was a time of innocence for us.

I don't really know that my experiences with work or for that matter, with play were much different than lots of other kids of the period...it seems to me that all of my friends had jobs, delivering papers early on and in some sort of part time employment afterwards either on a regular basis or during the summer or holidays. Everyone did something then partly because it was patriotic and partly because we all wanted to "hustle" to make a buck. It was in a way distracting from the main purpose of our lives...which was to get a good educational experience in order to be competitive when we went to college; but those part time jobs served an important educational purpose in their own right. Some of the lessons I learned about the trades that I plied or about the businesses that I was involved in remain in my mind today and were of considerable use to me in later life. As to playing, I don't think we differed from other generations of kids....except perhaps in terms of what could only be called an extraordinary innocence. None of the AZA boys smoked or got drunk (nor did our friendly (and virginal) BBG girls) and our leisure activities such as they were, were remarkably directed at what at the time and since could only be called "good clean fun". As described above it may have seemed a bit Victorian in morality (Queen Victoria must have had a

Jewish mother!) and frenetic in pace... but it was good times for us...even in war time Pittsburgh... and in retrospect I don't think I or any of my friends would have wanted to change it.

Boys and Girls Together:

I suppose in all of nature the most primal urge (after staying alive) is to reproduce the species; and the best documented and most clearly defined expression of that in all of history is the "mating dance" of adolescent males and females. Our generation was no exception and I think that it would be inappropriate of me to even suggest that the people on Crombie Street and my friends and fellow classmates at Taylor Allderdice did not hear the music or begin to make the moves of that wonderful dance. But just as with every generation there were some modifying factors that made our dance a little different from that of our parents or even more so perhaps, of our children.

First, despite what people say about the times, the late 30's and early 40's were a time of innocence for teen age children...and innocent we were. We derived information about sex from novels (never very explicit) and from whispered conversations with our peers (who sounded like they knew more but often knew less). There were no classes in sex education, no handbooks and no parental or even older sibling guidance. No one ever told me anything and I am sure that was the same for most of us. So, we all had a lot of misconceptions. Second was our fear of bad things happening. We knew about diseases (at least by name) and everyone feared "the clap" or "syph" but really didn't know why. What was perhaps even a greater threat was the enormous and overriding concern about an unwanted pregnancy...what a disaster that would be in say the 9th or 10th grade!

Then there was the thing about being Jewish. Jewish girls never went "all the way"....we could expect gluey open-mouthed kisses in the back seat of a car, tentative groping mostly through lots of clothes and what felt like a brassiere made of cast iron...or touching a stocking top (and never on the first few dates).... but never, never "the real thing"! Early on in our lives we came to accept this sanctity of the Jewish females virtue as an absolute; along with the inevitable development of "lover's stones" which produced such terrible pain in our dependent parts as to make us walk slowly to the door with our lady consorts and cry as we crawled back to go home. We fantasized that one of these virtuous ladies would suddenly turn into a nymphomaniac and assault us with outrageous sexual demands...but it never happened even when we abandoned our traditional code and dated a "shicksa" (young usually nubile Gentile girl)...it just never happened!

Finally, the war made things different especially for the girls. The girls we knew in our classes were not interested in us...young boys, just beginning to shave, usually half a head shorter and unable to dance very well...but were absolutely fascinated by Servicemen in their 20's...tall, handsome and very charming wearing their uniforms and knowing smiles...we were just no competition for them! I guess it was OK to date one of us...but not to go somewhere where you would be seen and only as a last resort. The boys on the other hand lived a fantasy life...expecting any day to meet the wife of someone who was overseas who was desperate and feral in her demands for sexual favors....but alas, it never happened!

So with those constraints and they were very real....and almost universal amongst the boys and girls of 14 or so at Taylor Allderdice....we started to learn the "mating dance" or at least the 1942 Pittsburgh Jewish version of it. I learned about "Spin the Bottle" and "Post Office" from the girls next door...not much fun and I didn't know that any of us knew why we were doing that. My very first "real" kiss came when I was 13 and took young lady name Soralee home from a Bar Mitzvah party one evening and she asked me if I wanted to kiss her goodnight....I thought about it and then did it...it was nice...and so was she. Somewhere around the age of 14 or 15 I began talking to my "girl friends"... especially Sonie Silverman, Estelle Rosenberg, Bernice Danovitz and Marcella Morowitz to mention a few, and occasionally we would sort of go out together but not for a real date. They were all interested in older men preferably in the Service so it was all sort of platonic. When I was 16 and learned how to drive I began to more seriously date and I started finding some younger girls who were interested in "older men" (namely me) and didn't mind if I didn't wear a uniform. We would go to Savers and dance for a few hours...the slow ones...and then back to Squirrel Hill to park in Schenley Park or in the heights overlooking Brown's Hill or on Beechwood Boulevard and "neck"...I would make some halfhearted attempts to get beyond the gluey kisses and the gropes and touches but would invariably be defeated by the restrictions imposed by several thousand years of belief in the essential frigidity of the Jewish woman and reverence for the sanctity of her virtue.

Did we all play by those rules? Pretty much I think. I am certain that some of the boys "did it" with some of the girls...and there were always rumors about a boy "making out" or a girl that "went all the way", but I think most of that was just the male animal baying in the wind out of frustration. I looked at my heroes and the admired "young-men-in-the-know" group and it seemed to me that they probably did get "the real thing" (all these phrases along with such expressions as "getting to first, second or third base" or "heavy petting", "putting out" or even cruder ones that I won't repeat were the universal sexual jargon of the time!) but I can't honestly vouch for it and I guess that's in a way what made them heroes...real heroes didn't "kiss and tell". We did learn a lot though particularly in terms of social relationship. We acquired a sophistication of sorts and some communication skills with the opposite sex...and a respect for virtue that I think is important but seems to have since fallen by the wayside. The boys and girls also learned a respect for each other (I hope it was mutual) which has been the model for all my relationships with women since. In retrospect those were the good things about our version of the mating dance. It wasn't all good, though...and I am afraid that some of us, boys and girls both felt inhibited by all the emotional baggage that we had to carry. I guess the concern lay in the possibility that somehow all of that could have altered our future ability to give and receive love...but as I think of them I believe that the people in our group were caring and confident enough to overcome any such deficit if it existed. They were then and are today in my mind...very special people!

The End of the War and the End of Youth:

At the end of the year of 1944 it was apparent that the Allies were winning the war. Rommel had been defeated in North Africa; and in Europe, we had successfully invaded Italy, Mussolini had been shot and hung and the Russians and the Russian winter had defeated the Germans on the Eastern Front. In the South Pacific, despite all the difficulties associated with multiple battle sites and the islands, we were closing in on the Japanese. The United States was tired of war...too many people had died, too much sacrifice, too much in cost of our resources. Pittsburgh was no exception...we read the paper avidly seeking evidence that the forces of Germany or Japan were ready for surrender.

Then it came...on Monday, May 7, 1945 the Germans surrendered...the Panzer divisions stopped and the mighty Wehrmacht laid down their arms. Pittsburghers were overjoyed ...celebrations happened spontaneously on the city streets and at Taylor Allderdice kids ran out of their classrooms into the halls shouting for joy. It wasn't quite over yet...the war in the Pacific still continued...but on August 6 and August 9 atomic bombs were dropped on Hiroshima and Nagasaki (an awesome event and little did we suspect how this would serve as a turning point in human history) and on Tuesday, the 14th of August the Japanese surrendered. We had won the war! What a great moment...I remember that we were at Colfax field when we heard... we sang and danced...parties were everywhere...girls kissing boys...boys kissing girls...people hugging Servicemen that they didn't know...everyone thrilled because the boys would soon come marching home...except... for those that died. Sadly, there were a lot of kids that didn't come home. Acquaintances, friends, classmates, coworkers at my various jobs, basketball players, people I had met along the tortuous course of our growing-up-days...were dead...struck down in their prime in some corner of the world with an unpronounceable name where no one knew them and few cared that their young hearts no longer beat and that their beautiful dreams of their future had died with them. Taylor Allderdice has erected a plaque on the wall of what used to be the Shady Avenue main entrance (there has been some remodeling so I am not sure it is an entrance anymore) which lists the names of all the kids that died between 1941 and 1945. It is a tragically long list and there are just too many friends there. I cried when I saw it and cry now when I think of it.

What about Crombie Street...what had happened to us during the war?
Hymie and Mary had grown older and to me as I looked at them, they no longer seemed indefatigable and invincible. My father's pace had slowed perceptibly and by 1945 he had angina and was just becoming disabled by it. There was no real treatment for angina at the time other than nitroglycerine and for him as it was for his brothers it was the beginning of his downward cardiac spiral (his took a lot longer than his

brothers...Hymie was 82 when he died...22 years after the onset of his angina!). Mary on the other hand continued to arise at 5:00 AM, clean the house, do the laundry (we now had what passed for a washing machine...vintage 1940!), sweep the porch and work in the garden....before she went to the store to work all day. The iron lady was however beginning to fray...after all in 1945 she was almost 60. In the winter evenings sometimes, she would sit in front of the radiator in the living room with a shawl (which I believe was her mother's) on her shoulders and doze...

Milt came back to Pittsburgh in 1944 to go to Dental School under the auspices of the ASTP program and he brought a wonderful surprise...his wife Cecille....what a charmer! Cecille was from Fort Worth and quite extraordinary in her beauty. She moved into Pittsburgh and our family...it couldn't have been easy for her...and managed her life with Milt (not the easiest person to deal with) and her three children remarkably well. Milt went back into the business (Specialty Clothing Company conquers all!) and even while he was in Dental School at Pitt, he worked weekends in the store.

Arthur "escaped" from Pittsburgh during the war...after his undergraduate work at Pitt he went to the University of Minnesota for graduate school in Physics and created a life for himself outside of ours. He never returned to Crombie Street or Pittsburgh except to visit. In Minneapolis, he met Shirley ...a truly remarkable, bright and very sweet lady who to her final day remained all those things plus mother to four children (and a fifth child, Arthur, if you asked her!). I remember once in the summer, during the war visiting Arthur and Shirley in Minneapolis before they were married. I was about 14 or 15 at the time and we all went out for the day on Lake Minnetonka...and I paddled a canoe while they sat on a seat in the middle of the craft urging me on. That trip was very special to me...I took the train to

Minneapolis by myself (including a scary change at Union Station in Chicago!) and felt very grown up!

Rita and Phyllis Solomon grew up...Rita continuing to be a bit shy and retiring and Phyllis a little wild and flamboyant; Selma Rogal became a lady...and a very nice one indeed; Leroy Weiner remained my true friend until he died of lymphoma a few years ago. The AZA boys continued to play together through college days then drifted apart...some moving to other parts of the world. The face of Crombie Street changed some. The neighbors built up their homes and there were several new houses constructed. At some point (I can't really remember when) the cobblestone street was converted to asphalt. With Arthur and Milt both out of the house, 6307 Crombie Street was suddenly roomy enough and except when we had visitors like my cousin Mary from Erie (who spent hours in our only bathroom) it was comfortable for the three of us.

In June of 1946, we had our Senior Prom...I took my then current "flame"...a really intelligent and nice person, Norma Sue Goodman. It is hard to forget that scene. The Prom was held in the Ballroom of the William Penn Hotel...Pittsburgh's finest. The lights were dim...I had rented a tuxedo (I think my first!)...Norma was wearing a powder blue strapless evening gown and looked wonderful. The members of the Senior Class danced slow dances to an orchestra and smiled and waved to one another as we circled the floor. I believe many of them thought (as I did) of friends, of our past few years together and most importantly the future. It was for us, a magical but sobering moment...the end of high school days...the end of our youth.

After graduation, I went on to Pitt along with what seemed like thousands of returning veterans who entered college under the GI bill. I lived at home at Crombie Street, still saw some of the old friends, studied in the basement of the house, watched that new medium...television, travelled to AZA tournaments, played basketball and began dating as a serious pursuit. But all of it was a little different now...I had lost some of the wonderment and innocence of my youth.

When I visited Pittsburgh for my son's graduation from Pitt Medical School (was I ever a proud father!) we came a day early to see him act and sing in their class show. The show was held in the auditorium at Taylor Allderdice High School....it was the first time that I had been back in many years. I sat in that auditorium and a part of me watched the show...but my mind wandered back to 1946. The auditorium made me remember Marshall Levy and Nancy Freedman playing the piano duet, the Choral Group singing a Christmas medley; the pep rallies before the football games, the class plays that occurred twice a year.... but I especially remembered that day when Orchestra A played the Processional as we marched in wearing cap and gown (complete with Allderdice green and white tassels on our caps) to our own graduation ceremony. I could really hear Mr. McClymonds say those words that I had heard so many times before... "Classes come and classes go and after a while they all merge into one..." I looked up at the words above the stage " Know Something; Do Something; Be Something" and I suddenly knew that Mr. McClymonds was wrong....we were different....we were special....we were creative...we were beautiful....we were the Class of 1946...and we did have a significant effect on our world.

Above – Hymie and Mary enjoying an allergy break (date unknown).
Below – The house at 6307 Crombie Street, Pittsburgh

Above – Henry as a camp counsellor, ca. 1945
Below – Taylor Allderdice High School

The Mankin Brothers (l. to r. Arthur, Henry and Milton) and their brides (l. to r. Shirley, Carole, Cecille), 1952

Henry and Carole on their wedding day, August 20, 1952

The beloved first Susie with Keith, Allison and David (l. to r. above) and Henry (below)

Above – Carole holds court in the early '60's
Below – Carole and Henry abroad (ca. 2005)

Two watercolors by the author:
Above – The Apollo Theater, Harlem, NY, 1958
Below – Pittsburgh, The Three Rivers, ca. 1964

99

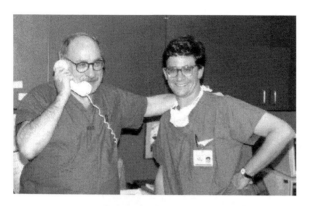

Above – Henry the teacher with his son and student, Keith, ca. 1994
Below – Henry, with his mother looking on, 2012

CHAPTER 4: IN MEDICAL SCHOOL

In 1993, I had just returned from attending my fortieth Medical School Reunion celebration. Our class which graduated in June 1953 reconvened in Pittsburgh for a weekend of what proved to be a series of sentimental greetings and strange feelings of unaccustomed group affection...triggered in my case and I'm sure for others as well by a kindling of memories of some long ago times and reminiscences regarding events that most of us had placed far back in our minds.

Before we left for Pittsburgh in thinking about the Reunion, Carole and I anticipated that the weekend would be exciting...an opportunity to see faces that we hadn't seen in some cases for forty years...to see what happened to each other since we marched up to get our diplomas in our black gowns and green hoods. In another way however there was a sense of foreboding...not just about the pain of loss of the class members that had died (and there has been an inordinate number of those...) but about seeing each other not as we are in our minds... bright, shining mid-twenties to mid-thirties people who were about to conquer the world...but the way we are.... old people...either desperately clinging to middle age or accepting the fact of entry into the final phases of life. I was concerned about giving and receiving the answers to the inevitable questions...what happened to our lives, our careers and our dreams? Could we by looking at each other and conversing for a few hours at dinner tables or on the inevitable tour of the medical school, even to a slight degree catch a glimpse of what we have all gone through...triumphs and defeats, hopes and despair, joys and tragedies?

As I remember us we all met early in September of 1949 partly in the Deans office in Old Mellon Institute as we lined up in Miss Glenn's office to register or all together for the first of many sessions in the Anatomy Laboratory in Pennsylvania Hall way up the hill... as we stood in line to get our coats, equipment and cadaver assignments for the gross anatomy class. It was a time of nervously looking at each other...seeking a familiar face...trying to seem confident in greetings with strangers who looked equally ill at ease. It was easy for me to identify with acquaintances from Taylor Allderdice days...all a little older than me. The Squirrel Hill group included Marshall Levy, Irwin Schaeffer, Paul Rogal, Mervin Stewart, Murray Weber and Bob Hepner. All except Murray were a year or more ahead of me in school and some had had a year or so of teaching in undergrad biology labs. I knew Dick Adler from AZA basketball ...he was from McKeesport and he quickly introduced me to Mel Cohen whose father ran a drugstore in Millvale. This incidentally just about completed the roster of Jewish members of the class...add in Lloyd Horne, Bobby Lewine and Ruth Powell and there we were! The majority of the class members however were older and unknown to me...and indeed more than a little intimidating...many were veterans of the war; or people who had worked in labs or undergrad departments for a long time waiting for the privilege of entering this Class of 1953. Some of them were by my standard at least, quite mature...meaning I suppose in their 30s. I remember a few "stand outs" ...people I couldn't help noticing from that first day...Earl Davis... Joe Riggio...Ray Peters ...Annie Stitt...Bob Good...Bob Sarver ...Marie Adelle Reagan ...class members who stood out because of their age or grace or seeming ease of social contact (which may tell a lot about me...at the time, I considered myself too young, relatively graceless and insecure in social situations!).

I don't recall much about "orientation" aside from the sharply etched images of all of us meeting on that first day. I vaguely remember Dean McElroy saying a few words to us ...I think it was on the first day but it is hard to picture where it occurred and what was said. I don't think our Dean was a memorable figure...I do somehow remember that he along with some others developed an assay for glucose and that he had a full head of straight black hair and was a heavy smoker! On the other hand I (and I suspect all of my classmates) clearly recall the meeting with Davenport Hooker surrounded by his staff in the histology lab...and his telling us about the rigors of the anatomy course and what we would have to do to survive in that first year (some of us didn't...like poor Bob Hepner or Nobby Dobrowalski).

It was in many ways a different age then...Pittsburgh was just returning to a peace time setting and winding down from a long period of high productivity in the mills and the excitement of being an integral part of the war effort. The veterans had returned...not the way they were when they left...nor were things the same as when they marched off to defend their country. A lot of them entered college under the GI bill and comprised a large component of our class as they would for several classes to come. It was a period of change. Pittsburgh before the war was an ugly city that just barely survived the depression...blackened by coal and grime from the mills and populated by ethnic groups many of whom spoke little English and clung tightly to their old-country traditions. The city was dominated by the heavy handed industrial barons who after extracting fortunes from the coal, iron and glass, gave a small measure back in the form of parks, libraries, universities and hospitals....and in addition creating great ugly mansions where they lived.

All of that began to change with the end of the war and the return of the veterans. Pittsburgh entered a period of prosperity as a result of defense spending and the jobs created by the war and began a long overdue face lift...building new and rather extraordinary monuments to industry (the downtown renaissance and Gateway Center had just begun); establishing strong and soon to become academic universities (Pitt, CIT which later became CMU and Duquesne were the big three); and cleaning not only the grimy buildings but the air...and indeed the city became brighter not just in appearance but in spirit. The ethnic groups began to Americanize (but not enough to lose their clannishness...or for that matter their charm) and the city took on a veneer of sophistication which in fact suited it...but which at least at first seemed to make its inhabitants a bit uncomfortable.

It was at the beginning of this rapid period of change that the Class of '53 first met in Oakland and started the great four year adventure of medical education...and it was indeed an adventure for all of us.

The University of Pittsburgh School of Medicine circa 1949 was a really remarkable educational institution....and as one might expect in almost all ways completely different from the current structure that bears the same name. Its avowed purpose seemed to be to train general practitioners for western Pennsylvania and most of the students came from that region. Furthermore any thoughts that the graduates might have about leaving the tristate area were discouraged. I remember Rube Snyderman once saying to me when I expressed an interest in interning at the University of Chicago that I can go if I wish but don't ever expect to come back to Pittsburgh. Specialty training outside of internal medicine was de-emphasized to say the least; and in fact the role models for specialists were in many cases sub-optimal. I believe that the number of generalists or at least primary care physicians in our class far exceeded that for classes from other Medical Schools in the eastern states. The tuition was low...I think it was $250.00 a trimester in our last year (unbelievable in comparison with the current over $50,000 per year!). There were no dormitories...it was assumed that most of the students would either live at home if they were unmarried; or for the older married members of the class that they would find an apartment in nearby Oakland or Shadyside or Squirrel Hill.

The basic science faculty were fairly standard for the times...some quite famous as it turned out. Drs. Hooker, Donaldson, Priman and Humphrey in Anatomy, Kruse, McLain and Ruhe in Physiology, Marie Fisher and Joe Quashnock in Chemistry and Aaron Stock, Leo Criep and even Jonas Salk taught us Microbiology. As to the clinical faculty only a small number were full time...or even received any funding at all from the Medical School. By and large these were the clinical scientists and included such individuals as Campbell Moses of the Addison Gibson Labs, Ted Danowski, Frank Mateer and the Renziehausen Group, E. R. McCluskey and Stuart Stevenson in Pediatrics, Henry Brosin and Bill Early in Psychiatry and Sam Harbison in Surgery. All of the remaining faculty were for the most part unpaid private practitioners from the hospitals. The degree of interest, clinical abilities and talent for education varied widely amongst this broad group of teachers and sometimes wc

105

were greeted with genuine enthusiasm and taught with great skill ...and at other times it was quite clear that our presence was considered a burden. It should be noted however that during our four year tenure the school made a few really daring moves ...recruiting Frank Dixon to head pathology, Klaus Hoffman in Chemistry, Albert Ferguson Jr. to chair the Orthopaedic service and Henry Brosin and his group in Psychiatry. That was the beginning of the move to develop a committed full time academic group which ultimately led to the outstanding faculty at the University today.

Another feature of the 1949 Pitt Medical School which was very striking was its remarkable "alphabetization" of the student activities. When we all met in the Anatomy Lab on the second floor of Pennsylvania Hall in September of 1949, four of us in strict alphabetical order were assigned to a cadaver; so that George Makdad and I were on one side of the table (the right) and John Marlowe and Charles Mason on the left. When we looked at the table on our right, we saw Francis McArdle, John McCague, Bill McCall and Larry Madden; while on our left was Jim Medley, Mike Miklos, Norm Miller and Bob Milligan...and so it went. That seemed appropriate for anatomy perhaps for ease of identification of the students by the prosecting faculty, but it became apparent that the same alphabetized ordering of things occurred in many of our other courses. The "M"s stuck together for four years; as did the "R"s and the "C"'s, etc. and mostly the groups not only became involved with each other in a daytime setting but in many cases studied together, ate their meals together and became socially friendly. It was fascinating to watch for this at our reunions and find that even after 40 years "birds of a letter flocked together"; and Irv Schaeffer, Dave Schaub and Joe Scarlet had almost as much to talk to each other about as Don Cope, Bob Cott and Mel Cohen or Joe Riggio, Marie Adelle Reagan and Ed Radasky.

There were events in each of the years that none of us can ever forget...and perhaps sharing memories of these was the basis for our kinship and sense of camaraderie when we met on our 40th anniversary. They weren't cataclysmic events...or even unusual in the lives of medical students then or today, but some of them may have been a bit unique to our class. Pre-clinical teaching occurred in the Old Mellon Institute and that's where the labs were (who can forget the smoked drums in Physiology or Ruhe running up the stair...or Aaron Stock telling us about Miss Bailey's hormone broth!) except for anatomy and histology education which took place in Pennsylvania Hall. We had a full two trimesters of anatomy and each day pretty much started way up the hill. If you came to work on the street car, it was really a walk...particularly in the winter; if you drove we were allowed to park in the lot behind Presbyterian (now Scaife Hall!) and it was still a walk. Afternoons took place for the most part in Mellon or in Presbyterian and walking down was easier. Faculty and students...we met and interacted in that first two years in what was considered appropriate behavior for the time. We wore ties and coats to school...we had exams which terrified us (it seemed to me that they occurred almost weekly!)....we laughed at the appropriate times and sometimes inappropriately at what seemed to us to be some very funny things...as when Jesse Wright lectured about painful balls (after the first time she said it she left out the words "of the feet")....or when some wag, I don't remember who, told us the "never lower Tillie's pants.." mnemonic for the bones of the carpus! We memorized enormous lists of structures in anatomy and neuroanatomy (I still can't get some of them especially the mnemonics, like "the lingual nerve took a swerve..." out of my head!) and were constantly testing ourselves or each other. "What is the origin, insertion, nerve and blood supply of the rectus femoris?" became a challenge; and if an answer didn't spring to our lips we suffered some mild tachycardia, beads of sweat and perhaps even a sleepless night! We were bottomless pits of countless seemingly independent bits of information...of little use by themselves. Somehow we knew that they would ultimately make sense and have application to human disease...and we suffered through the first two years living for that moment of revelation. Pitt like most schools of the time believed that "pre-clinical" meant just that...and it wasn't until the end of the second year that we all went to the Falk Clinic and were taught what was then and still is a part of the art of medicine, physical diagnosis (alas, with the advent of newer imaging techniques, many fear that it will soon be a lost art!). We learned new and wondrous words for our vocabularies ..."diastolic murmur"..."rales"..."Babinski's sign" ... "alopecia" ..."borborygmi"..."waterhammer-pulse"..."Argyll-Robertson pupil"; and now happily memorized new lists: the components of the Horner's syndrome; or the characteristic articular signs in rheumatoid arthritis; or the reflex alterations in hemiplegia. This was why we were here...the stuff we had dreamed about! We now carried stethoscopes and reflex hammers and ophthalmoscopes...and didn't always correct patients when they called us by that magic appellation "Doctor"!

It should be evident from the foregoing that the clinical years were more satisfying to our driving desire to become caretaking physicians, but at Pitt these last two years were really quite complicated. There were 100 people in the class (several had dropped out in the first and second years but we added a few from other schools or from the labs to keep the numbers up) and not all could have the same experience. Presbyterian, Children's and Magee were central, the latter for Obstetrics and Gynecology but really principally for the opportunity to meet Dr. James Delevan Heard...one of our most extraordinary and impressive teachers that any of us had ever met (none of us had ever stood when a teacher entered the room before this and I daresay none have since!). It isn't hard to remember those lessons in diagnosis even after 40 years.

Because of the size of our class, however for our medical and surgical clerkships (both junior and senior) we had to rotate through one of several "off campus" hospitals. These included Allegheny General, Montefiore, St. Francis and Mercy Hospitals and each was different in orientation and quality of not only the educational experience but such important ancillaries as food (Mercy was best!), ease of transport (Montefiore and Mercy were a direct shot on the streetcar tracks) and house officer complement and interaction (Montefiore and Allegheny General seemed best for these but often a toss-up). The key issue was the faculty. If you were at Presby you had Lucien and Frank Gregg and the Danowski group for Medicine and Sam Harbison, the Watsons and Bernie Fisher for surgery...and it was generally pretty academic. The cases were more complex and the workups sometimes tortuous ...and the medical student was more often an observer rather than a participant. The Departments of Medicine and Surgery at Mercy and St. Francis were much busier it seemed to me with less esoteric cases and much more opportunity for the student to do things such as work in the Emergency Room (Mercy's was really busy!), sew up lacerations, scrub in on cases, do lumbar punctures, draw bloods, etc. Montefiore was somewhere in between but was considerably smaller than the others and less active. The key problem with these four affiliated hospitals was that the teaching staff didn't always teach...or even answer questions ...and when they did it seemed to some of us, that they didn't always have the right answers. We got used to that somehow.

Pediatrics was special. The time at Children's Hospital was valuable principally because of the spectacular teaching efforts of Stuart Stevenson, Paul Gaffney, Bert Girdany and some of the others. Some lessons about children really struck a chord for some of us...it was at Children's that I first saw a child die and I don't think I will ever forget that.

The teaching sessions and shorter clerkship periods for the specialty services were equally remarkable...each in their own way. We had a week or two on urology where we learned about catheters and prostatic massage; spent our requisite times on the Obstetrical Service at Magee and each did a delivery (great stuff!); had a weekly session on Orthopaedics at Allegheny General for six weeks or more in the senior year, where we were exposed to the extraordinary show put on by Paul Steele and his gang of gorillas (it's a wonder that three of our class ended in Orthopaedics!); spent some time on neurosurgery where some of our class were intrigued by the drama of brain surgery as practiced by a flamboyant Paul Bragdon or a technically competent Stuart Rowe (two of my fellow "M"s, Miklos and Mooney ended up in Neurosurgery); learned a completely new language in ophthalmology and otolaryngology...both at Eye and Ear and attractive to some (at least three of our class went into ophthalmology); and of course spent a seemingly inordinate length of time in psychiatry which drew a lion's share of the specialty time and really attracted a large number of our class...perhaps more than any field except Obstetrics and General Practice. The teaching of psychiatry both at Western Psychiatric Institute and St. Francis was quite thorough and the ward time useful and in some ways fascinating. Our time at Western not only gave us the opportunity to learn about the dark corners of the patient's minds, but gave the members of that department a chance to look at us. Bill Early was particularly intrigued with the psychopathology of medical students and we presume that he obtained ample new data from the class of 1953!

That was the way it was for the clinical rotations...a schedule published by the Dean's office every trimester which announced our rotations, more or less "alphabetized"...we read it sometimes with profane complaint ... but off we went. Transport was a problem for some of us without cars so that the "M"s at least and I presume the others as well did a lot of car-pooling. We would meet at our first location....be it Presby or Mercy or wherever and then pile into the cars of a few (Mooney was our most constant driver) and head for the next hospital. The entire class met together several times a week at Mercy (who can forget the unforgiving seats in the amphitheater!) or Magee (much easier to fall asleep!) or Presby or occasionally St. Francis for lectures some of which were exciting and interesting and others pretty bad. Remarkably the attendance was pretty good at those sessions even for bad lecturers in bad weather...I guess we were compulsive about attendance at classes but in truth, I think we really had a quest for knowledge. We all took copious notes ...and poured over them before exams. If you asked us now about those notes I would guess that a lot of us (including me!) saved them....I am not sure why...perhaps as a dusty monument to our life and times at Pitt.

Studying was another facet of our student life. Amongst the 100 members of the class I am sure every possible method of study was tried with variable success. Some studied at home every evening ....either alone or with a partner....others spent hours in the library....some went to bed upon return home from classes, woke at midnight and studied all night...others gathered in pre-examination groups ranging from 3 to 10 for an all-night orgy of questions and answers laced with black coffee and cigarettes. Everyone studied....everyone learned...some faster than others but we all passed the exams and had the answers for class. It wasn't easy though. I can still remember as can I am sure many of my classmates the notes, the books, the questions, the phone calls in the night seeking a missed point....and the fatigue that accompanied it all.

To add to the burden of a life of classes and study and daily travel, some of us moonlighted in our senior year in the local hospitals (drawing bloods at Presby, doing histories and physicals at Eye and Ear or covering the Emergency Rooms or floors at hospitals which had no interns...South Side, Braddock or even New Kensington!). I can't imagine how we were covered for malpractice at the time...and I am not even sure we had insurance of any sort...but those were different times....far less litigious for one thing. Most of us who did these things said we were doing it for the money... (some of the jobs paid handsomely) but in truth for all of us, it was another opportunity to try our hand at medicine....at caretaking...at responding to emergencies. We just couldn't get enough of the heady challenges associated with responding to the needs of the sick.

Was it all work? Of course not. We had lives outside of medical school and did all the recreational things that others did...perhaps less frequently and with more intensity. The summers were ours (I worked as a counsellor in a summer camp for several years) as were the weekends (parties, dates and the usual). We had sports activities as participants or spectators (Forbes Field wasn't far away...nor was Pitt Stadium!). Many of the older members of the class were married and some like myself married during the clinical years...in fact over half the class were married by the time we graduated. I think that helped to keep us sane....but maybe contributed to the insanity of our partners!

The four years seemed forever when we went through them but in truth looking back they flew by like moments. We had our graduation on the lawn at the Cathedral of Learning on the Heinz Chapel side and marched up to the podium for our diplomas in our Pitt blue and gold trimmed gown and our green hoods. A very special moment for us and our families...a milestone...a passage...an experience to savor. It was a commencement in the true sense of the word...a beginning of a career soon to be followed by an internship, a residency and then practice...and a very special and rewarding life of service to humanity.

So 40 years later our group gathered to commemorate that day in 1953 when our careers began. Out of 99 class members we had 30 who attended, 23 who had responded but couldn't attend, 16 who didn't respond and alas, 20 who had died. Of the 30 who attended fully half were either completely or partially retired. A look at this overall record for the Class of '53 is sobering to say the least.

Despite the dreary statistics however it was a special occasion. Greetings were great....and the conversation was remarkable. We talked of the bygone days in the Medical School; of our lives in these 40 years; of our successes and regrets. We remembered our faculty and reminded ourselves of the good teachers (and some of the bad ones) and recalled moments in education that were indelibly etched in our memories....Dr. Heard's lectures, WWG McLachlan's rounds, Ted Danowski's laboratory, Paul Steele's roll call, Tom Mabon's tour of the water purification plant, Henry Brosin's case discussions, Tryphena Humphrey's exposition on the nervous system (thank God for the blizzard that wiped out the final examination) and many, many more. We had some moments of sadness when we saw the list of 20 lost friends and heard of the illnesses of some of the others. It was indeed a shock to see each other as we are now...but not as bad as I thought it would be...and although some of us seemed to be caricatures of the way we looked in our class pictures, there were identifiable features that were unchanged...a gait pattern, a smile, a facial expression or a way of speech that reminded us of our four years together so long ago.

On the Wednesday or Thursday before our group met for our reunion on Friday night, Mervin Stewart (who must be complimented and thanked for single-handedly arranging the entire Reunion), called me to ask that I say a few words at the dinner on Saturday night. I put together some notes on Saturday afternoon after the tour of the Medical School (really amazing how things have changed) and the city (talk about changes!); and after Ross Musgrave gave us greetings from the Dean and the Alumni Association, I said my few words, badly I fear but like many things in my recent life with considerable feeling. What I tried to convey was as follows:

> "Forty years is a long time...and much has happened in medicine since we graduated....some of it would be quite unbelievable to us when we were students and even to our faculty. In fact, almost nothing is the same as it was when we were in school and enormous strides have been made in the healing of the sick.
>
> The diseases are different....we have lost polio and gained AIDS (given the choice, I think most of us would want polio back!); and tuberculosis which dominated our medical school days (can we all remember learning percussion and auscultation on the patients at Leech Farm TB sanitarium?) was almost gone...but has now returned with a vengeance in a drug resistant form. Rheumatic fever is virtually gone and pneumococcal pneumonia which in McLachlan's day killed 50% of the patients is now treated along with most other infections with antibiotics and without hospitalization. Cardiac disease is curable (it wasn't then) and liver flaps and St. Vitus Dance rarely happen anymore.
>
> Diagnostic techniques are different...the list of new lab tests are extraordinary not

to mention, quite acronymic and alphabetical. We now have access to CEA, ANA, PSA, SGOT, SGPT, IEP, HLA and many more...and can count of such wonders as 5' nucleotidase, osteocalcin, 1,25 dihydroxy-vitamin D and a whole host of c-DNA probes to define disease states and patient status with exquisite accuracy. Unbelievable events in imaging have occurred as well. The Class of '53 had X-rays and maybe angiography. We now have radionuclide scanning, ultrasound, Doppler's, CT and the fabulous MRI to image and illuminate and define the nature and extent of disease in spectacular detail.

Treatment modalities are different....in 1949, if it didn't respond to penicillin or streptomycin or it couldn't be surgically excised, we couldn't do much for our patients' diseases. Now we have Xantac which has pretty much put the ulcer surgeons out of business...and Prozac which has done the same for the psychoanalysts! There's a new antibiotic almost monthly (unfortunately the bacteria seem to keep pace with our discoveries) and we can cause a diuresis in almost anyone, keep people with renal failure alive for years with dialysis, correct their hypercalcemia, bring their soaring blood pressure into range, calm their tender joints, control their arrhythmias, replace their missing enzymes and soon will be able to alter their gene structure. Surgery too has undergone some magnificent changes in 40 years. Microsurgery, organ transplants, balloon angioplasty, minimally invasive arthroscopy, culdoscopy, mediastinoscopy, peritoneoscopy, endoscopic cholecystectomy are now done routinely in all our hospitals and the laser and robotics are on the horizon. Who would have dreamed of all this in 1953?

The amazing thing is that all of this has happened over forty years and it is clearly a tribute to our scientists who have made these discoveries and to our clinicians who have applied them so wondrously to help suffering mankind. The world is a far better place because of these spectacular events in our history and people who live longer and have far better lives provide daily testimony to our success as a discipline.

There is another amazing thing however in all of this which is really when you think about it, almost as startling. The fact is that we, the Class of '53 have kept up with all of this! We have gone from kids who listened to each other's hearts with stethoscopes in 1950 to people who are able to interpret echo-cardiograms and thallium stress tests; from fledgling physicians using a percussion hammer to determine the presence or absence of an intracranial lesion to people who are comfortable reading an EEG report or looking at an MRI or CT of the brain. We can interpret lab tests, follow our patients with the most complex of tools and if we are surgeons perform feats daily that none of us or our faculty ever thought possible forty years ago. How on earth did we do this?

Well, I think the answer lies in the evident truth that we did in fact get a very good education forty years ago...not just in memorized lists of anatomical facts or symptom complexes or even of drugs to use for which disease...but in learning about learning ...in developing a pattern for a lifetime of trying to find better ways...in establishing a curiosity about disease and when there were no answers trying to find one. We developed that capacity sometimes because of good teachers ...sometimes despite bad teachers...but always I think because we, the Class of '53 taught each other how to learn.

So in conclusion of this rather rambling retrospective of our forty years, this reunion is in fact a tribute to us, the Class of '53... successes in the arts and sciences of medicine and the best teachers any of us have ever had. We did it all for forty years for our patients, for our families and in truth for ourselves ...and we did it all well... and in my humble opinion with extraordinary style and grace."

CHAPTER 5: LIFE WITH CAROLE AND THE KIDS IN LOTS OF PLACES

Memories of the early days for Carole and Henry:

Sweet Carole and I first met at Christmas time in the year 1950....Paul and Sonny Rogal at that time were very involved with each other. Paul was a classmate of mine at Pitt medical school and Sonny was a classmate of Carole's at BU. They wanted me to meet Carole, so I went to Boston for Christmas and New Years to meet her. Before I went, I sent her a picture of a dog and indicated that that was me... I think she thought that that was silly and that I was silly, too   I was only 22 that year and she was 19 years of age.

I stayed in a place at Washington Square and went to her home to see her and meet her mother and father and cousin Ira Mogul and Aunt Sally and her Grandmother...and then we went out every day and night...the last time to the home of a friend of Ira's for New Year's Eve.   I thought she was very smart and quite attractive but we really weren't crazy about each other...I did like her father and mother, though ...a couple of class act people and the apartment at 1963 Commonwealth was sort of interesting. Carole and I did do some necking (an old term from the 40s and 50s) but not much else. I went home and promised to write and did with thanks and with news, etc. several times.

Anyway, that was the beginning and then for some reason a few months later around Valentine's Day in 1951, I wrote a letter to her saying...is there any reason to keep corresponding? We really don't have much in common, etc.   She replied that I shouldn't give up that quickly so I invited her to my Med School Fraternity Party. She couldn't come because of exams but asked if I would come to her Sorority Dinner Dance...and I decided that I would...and I did. I didn't know it but when Carole had the measles she and Sonny decided that I was the guy she wanted to marry and they put together the list of people they were going to invite to the wedding. Anyway, I came to the party and it was a great event! And guess what...we fell in love! I am still not sure why that happened but it was almost instantaneous and mutual. We looked at each other and smiled and hugged and kissed and we both knew that it would be for life! The trip was interrupted though because my father Hymie had a heart attack and I had to fly home and leave my car in Boston. When I came back to get my car, that was when we decided that we ought to get married!

Once we became engaged, I started going to Boston and to other places with her...for family events. Ira's wedding to Diane was a special family affair and by then everyone knew that we were betrothed. At one point, while in Boston, I asked her father if I could marry her and he agreed that it would be a good thing. I met all the family folks, Alice and her crazy husband, Elmer and her son Eddie and, of course Diane's really crazy family.

So then we got married in the summer of 1952 after I finished my courses at Pitt to get my BS degree. It was a great wedding in Boston with all the families there (including my Aunt Rosie and my brother Milton and sister in law Cecille). I stayed at Sonny's mother's place the night before the wedding. Hymie and Mary smiled a lot although Mary had only met Carole once and wasn't sure that she was the right girl for me. The wedding was wonderful with Milton as my best man and Sonny as

Carole's matron of honor but we had the shortest honeymoon on record because Milton had to go somewhere on vacation and I had to cover for him at Hymie's store. So it was three days together before we moved back to Pittsburgh and drove there with Sonny and Paul. We moved in with Mary and Hymie for a week or so until we found an apartment and moved in and I began my final year at Pitt Medical School. Carole applied for and accepted two jobs...the first of these was with a Jewish community organization and the second with the Concordia Club. The heat died in our apartment home in the early spring so we had to move back into Crombie Street....not as bad as either of us expected. So that was the beginning of our marriage.

We had lots of friends in those days: Paul and Sonny Rogal, Marshall and Lois Levy, Mervin and Marcia Stewart, Irv and Marian Schaeffer, Mel and Mickey Cohen and other classmates and we were busy socially, as well as educationally for me, and at work for my bride.

Paul and I graduated in May of 1953 and before we started our Internships and separated we decided to drive to Miami for vacation. Sonny and Carole were thrilled and it was a great trip, although we didn't have very much money. We did swim (Sonny and I got sunburnt so we didn't do as much as Carole and Paul) and we ate out and wandered around. We drove back to Washington and let Paul and Sonny get a train back to Pittsburgh, where Paul was going to do his residency and then Carole and I went to Boston to bring her mother and father to my graduation. It was a very nice graduation on the park area in front of the Cathedral of Learning. I was listed as one of the top five in the class and won a prize. Mary had a party for us at a place in

East Liberty that served kosher food and it was a great time.

Internship in Chicago:

Carole and I arrived in Chicago in time to start my internship and particularly the indoctrination, which occurred on or about 26 June, 1953. We were able to get an apartment in a building not far from the University Hospital at 5401 South Ellis Avenue, which was small but satisfactory, with a kitchen, a living room and a bathroom (no bedroom...just a Murphy bed!). It was on the second floor of the building and we parked our car on the street. Arthur and Shirley already lived in Chicago and that was one of the nice things about it...we were able to see them and have an occasional dinner. They already had three children, Eric, Joan and Ruth...all cute and smart. Shirley was very pleasant and very helpful to Carole in getting things started.

I started the internship and shortly thereafter Carole started a job as a secretary for James Wood Johnson Carpenter MD a pioneer in radiation oncology. Carole claimed she had no typing skills but she was then as she is now, a good learner and Carpenter was very happy with her. I had a roommate, named Ray Lavender who was a good physician and I became very friendly with some of my internship classmates...Lou Cohen, Lester Dragstedt and Wayne Akeson to mention a few. We worked very hard and I enjoyed all aspects including obstetrics, gastro-intestinal disease, cardiology, general surgery but most of all orthopaedics. I ran into some really great people in the Orthopaedic Service, including Tom Brower and Bill Enneking and of course the Chief, Howard Hatcher. It was a great service, but it was last on my time in the program and I had already decided to

123

go into Internal Medicine and begin my residency in that discipline on July 1, 1954. I became interested partly because of Walter Palmer and Joseph Kirschner who were stimulating and exciting teachers in the Department of Medicine. One of my interns then was later a colleague in orthopaedic oncology, Ralph Marcove and I got to know him well.

Service in the Navy at Hawthorne Nevada...1955-57

All was going well in my residency until November of 1954 when I received a letter from the U.S. Navy. Either I accept a position as a Medical Officer in the Navy or I would have to report to Pittsburgh on January 1 to serve as an ordinary seaman. It was the end of the Korean War and I decided to become a Lieutenant Junior Grade in the Naval Medical Corps and see where I would have to go. These were not our happiest days. I had to buy a uniform, get some black shoes and a hat and then go to Great Lakes Naval Training Station at –20° below zero for my two-week indoctrination. When I received my assignment Carole and I were stunned...it was to the US Naval Ammunition Depot in Hawthorne, Nevada! Neither of us could imagine where or what that would be like! But we had little choice...we just got into the car with all our possessions on board and left Chicago to go to Hawthorne. We decided to go by way of a warmer route and chose to go to St. Louis and on from there via Route 66 all the way to California. We stopped in motels on the way and actually spent one day at the Grand Canyon. We were early in arriving so we decided to stop in Ventura to see Carole's uncle Jack and his really nice Panamanian wife Lee and that was fun, too. Then finally, we drove to Hawthorne and after a night in a Motel in that little town I went to the base and checked in! Carole expressed some real terror when I left her at the Motel and went to work, but fantastically, everything really worked out pretty well. We were given an apartment first as a temporary site until a house opened up and then we had a very nice house with a living room, kitchen, bedroom and dining area. The house had a garden (no joy for Henry!) and a nice porch. There was a house next door, where a very nice guy name Earl Carlson and his family lived...along with a really sweet dog named George. Lots of other people around us...Bob Parks, the dentist and his wife were across the street and a not so nice lawyer Preston Sawyer and his cranky wife were also there. Captain Richter was the commanding officer and Lars Anderson was his assistant. Jim and Mary Saxman were friendly with us and Don Aldine was a single person in the Officer's quarters and was loved by all the wives (except Carole!) and especially the nurses. Some others who joined us including Alan Adams and his wife Ollie and the Chief of Medicine at the Hospital where I worked, Dr. McCluskey, who I really think was a drunk, but a nice guy. Proctor Hug was a manager there, who later became a judge and I delivered his son along with Alan Adams' son and of course my daughter Allison. I did a lot of obstetrics since no one else could do it and I think I delivered 300 or so babies. Somewhere in the middle of the second year, Frank Tracy and his Canadian wife joined us. He was sort of a weirdo...with both dental and medical degrees, but not very good at either. I also spent some time with the Piute Indians and discovered that they had lots of tuberculosis and were really not very well treated by the Nevada government.

What did we do for fun in Hawthorne? Well, we ate out a lot and when we went into the town we gambled a little at the El Capitan Hotel and Restaurant. Another place that we ate and gambled a bit was called Joe's and there was also a great Chinese restaurant. We watched the waters flow in Walker Lake (only went swimming a few times, because it was a salt lake!) and looked at and sometimes partly climbed mile high Mt. Grant. There was the little town of Babbit close to the naval station where we shopped and where lots of our employees worked. I coached and played basketball with some of our Marines and Naval people and that was fun...we weren't very good, partly because we were too short of stature (Marines were at that time limited in height!). I also learned to fire guns there, particularly when the commanders and I decided I should be in the Fleet Marine Force rather than just the Navy.   We went to Reno sometimes for some time out and I actually made friends with a physician there. We also went to Carson City and Nellis Air Force base which was located in Fallon, the next town about 30 miles away. They didn't have a hospital so sent their patients to us. Another site not far away, which was at least partially occupied by Piute Indians was the town of Tonopah.

Carole and I spent some time in the officer's club on the base and established a bridge club. We won most of the time (no one else played very well!). The only other Jewish people then were not in the military...a husband and his wife, who we got to know pretty well...although they didn't want to admit that they were Jewish!   One of our nurses was called up to go somewhere else and told Carole she didn't know what to do with her dog; so Carole and I adopted Susie, a beautiful and loving black cocker spaniel. She was wonderful for us and loved Carole, Allison and me.   My in-laws Ann and Harold Pinkney came to visit us and they loved Allison and also Susie...it was clearly the beginning of a wonderful family!

At some point during our two years, it became apparent that I had to go back to a residency and I decided after my experience in Orthopaedics at the University of Chicago and the amount of orthopaedic care I gave patients in Hawthorne, that I would rather do that then go back into Internal Medicine. So I wrote to Dr. Hatcher and asked if I could do a residency with them. He replied that they didn't have a position but felt that if I wrote to Dr. Joseph Milgram at the Hospital for Joint Diseases, that they might have a place for me. I did and he replied yes...but it wouldn't start until July...but that I could spend 5 months with Henry Jaffe, the Chief of Pathology at HJD, before I started the program. Carole and I agreed and decided in late December to pack Allison, Susie and everything we owned into a new Chevrolet car that we had just bought and drive to New York to start a new life in the big city!

New York, New York, a helluva town from 1957 to 1960:

We drove and drove and stopped in Pittsburgh on the way; and then we arrived in New York City in early January and decided to try to find a residence. Neither of us had ever lived in New York before and we weren't sure where to live. Arthur was living there in Huntington on Long Island, so we decided that Queens might be a good place to go and were able to rent an apartment at 150-07 Jewel Avenue in Queens...actually I think it was called Forest Hills. The rent was $270.00 a month and we had a living room, two bedrooms, a dining area, a kitchen and a bathroom. It was on the first floor...so we had a little lawn outside (which was very nice for Susie) and there were three steps outside to get in. We had neighbors upstairs who were the people who maintained the place and they were very nice to be with. We parked the car on the street in front of the apartment or sometimes across the street...there were no meters then and parking was easy. Going to work from Queens was really quite simple then, although there was a toll on the Queensboro Bridge, but it was not very expensive. I got there easily every day and parked across from the Hospital in a parking space near a little park in East Harlem.

The Hospital and the doctors at HJD:

The Hospital for Joint Disease was a great facility. It was located at 124th and Madison Ave, right in the middle of East Harlem, across from a small park named Mt Morris Park. It was only one block away from the then fabulous 125th Street, which had many stores, theaters and apartment buildings. The old Apollo Theater was one of the most famous sites and still is today. Most of the people who lived and worked in that part of Harlem were black and although there was some problem with discrimination, the crime problems in the 1950s were relatively minimal and walking the streets even at night did not really disturb most of us.

The administrative director of the Hospital was Abraham Rosenberg who lived in an office on the first floor and was quite efficient. His desk was free of papers and he was generally knowledgeable about the problems of the Hospital. Amelia Mater was his administrative assistant and she did everything there, including taking care of the needs of the residents. She was very helpful to me when I arrived...as was Henry L. Jaffe, chief of Pathology who taught me a lot about orthopaedic disease in my five-month tour with him. He was a great man and was revered by the other members of the staff and indeed the world of Orthopaedic pathology.

In July of 1957, I started the Orthopaedic residency program with five other residents. They were Richard Smith, Joseph Conrad, Donald Goldberg, Henry Litchman and Marvin Chirls. We didn't get paid very much...I think it was only $60 a month but we got free meals and our uniforms were laundered without charge. We worked hard, taking care of large numbers of patients with polio and other kinds of strange diseases, helping the faculty operate, covering a busy emergency room which had lots of free care and trying to learn from the staff and each other. We were good at it too and the six of us turned out to be very good Orthopaedic surgeons. In our senior year, I was named Chief Resident and received some extra funding and by then I was also on the faculty of Hunter College where I taught some biology once a week. I also was in the Naval Reserve and went to monthly meetings and got paid for that and with my status as a veteran, I received an extra sum of $160 a month from the GI bill, which made all the difference in the world to Carole, Allison and by then a son, David and of course Susie as well.

I must at this point say a few words about our staff, who by and large were spectacular. Joe Milgram was a prince...he was knowledgeable, an excellent caretaker and loved to teach. Manny Kaplan was the best anatomist and hand surgeon anywhere and Joe Buchman took on all kinds of problems and was inventive and careful in his approach to some strange disorders. Leo Mayer was an icon...he knew a lot about polio and was widely quoted throughout the world. Barney Kleiger worked with him and was my friend. A strange guy named Paul Lapidus was the foot surgeon and really

129

revolutionized the care of major problems. Robert Milch was an inventive surgeon who didn't wear gloves (wow!) and Charles Sutro was a genius who contributed to our learning. Jacob Graham did a lot of spine surgery as did Kleinberg and some others. There were many others who contributed but two of the best were Albert Betcher, our chief of Anesthesia, and Alex Norman, our bone radiologist.

So, what did Carole and I do for fun in New York in the early days? First, we made friends with lots of people including especially my residency classmates. Carole got to know the wives of all of them...some like Jane Smith were a little hard to communicate with, but we all got along pretty well but we had some good times together. I guess we were most friendly with the Litchmans...Judy was very warm and pleasant and he was a nice guy. Arthur and Shirley Mankin lived in Huntington, Long Island at the time and we went to see them and their kids, Eric, Joan ("Queenie"), Ruthie and Daniel ("Bonky") regularly. We went out to dinner a lot usually in Manhattan and got to know and love some of the Jewish restaurants. We went to movies and even theater rather frequently for people who didn't have any money and saw some great shows such as Cabaret, My Fair Lady, West Side Story and The Sound of Music and even went to some concerts at Symphony Hall. Some of the faculty were friendly, especially Barney Kleiger and Herman Robbins and even Joe Milgram. It was good times for us...and then my sweet Carole gave birth to David. She had the baby at Forest Hills Hospital on Long Island and then we had the two kids to take care of ...as well as, of course, sweet Susie. We were young, and in love and in contrast with later years, we were tireless. I read, I taught, I wrote my first three papers, two with Barney

Kleiger and one with Jack Graham...sort of the beginning of my academic career. One of the things I remember was when I taught at Hunter College, I would come home at about 8:00 PM and would stop to get dinner for Carole and me ...good food, good times for sweet Carole and me. I also remember some bad times: having to go to Camp Lejeune for a week every year as part of my Fleet Marine Force training; and my six month period at Harrison S. Martland Hospital in Newark...I worked too hard and spent too much time away from home.

Anyway, it all ended in June of 1960...I received a certificate, became Board eligible and was ready to start a career in Orthopaedics...but what to do? I remember a colleague from Chicago days name Tom Brower, who had an academic job in Pittsburgh and I got in touch with him and asked if there were any opportunities there. He and Albert B. Ferguson agreed that they could use me for one year...to work for $11,000. We decided to do it and moved back to Pittsburgh in July of 1960 to start what proved to be the beginning of a very productive academic career.

Back to Pittsburgh and the University Orthopaedic Service

Carole and I arrived in Pittsburgh by car and we had to ask my father for a loan of $600 to pay for moving (I don't think we ever paid him back!). We were able to get a small house on Mark Drive in Verona (specifically 8014 Mark Drive), which incidentally had a number of friendly neighbors. Mervin and Marcia Stewart lived a few blocks away and Fred and Esther Marks three houses away. Lennie and Millie Schwartz lived next to Mervin but they weren't as friendly to us as the Stewarts and the Marks. Our kids discovered the two sweet Marks girls very soon and became friendly with Yedda Sue and Betsy but they really didn't have as much to do with the Stewart kids.

The house was small and designed and built by a guy named Calderelli. . It had two floors...the first floor had a living room, kitchen, dining room and three bed rooms...one for Allison, one for David and pretty soon, one for Keith who was born soon after we arrived at Magee Hospital (same place where I was born in 1928!). Carole had a mean obstetrician, Dr. Pink, who didn't think she was really in labor and hollered at her when she came into the hospital that August night, but was surprised when she delivered Keith shortly thereafter.

What did I do at Pitt Medical Center? The answer to that question is everything! I had an office in Children's Hospital next to those of Bob Ferguson and Tom Brower and some space in the Laboratory on the 9th Floor of the Medical School with Patrick Laing, located across from that of the rheumatologist Gerald Rodnan, who became a friend! I took care of patients in the office, on the Orthopaedic floor, in the Emergency Room, at Leech Farm tuberculosis sanitarium and some other places as well. I taught the residents and medical students diligently and with sometimes, great pleasure although I have to admit everyone worked so hard in those days that they didn't always stay awake. I did research on cartilage structure and in 1962, I received my first NIH grant and in fact was continuously funded until 2002!

Amongst the faculty, I made lots of friends including Bob and Louise Ferguson, Bill and Jean Donaldson, Patrick and Patricia Laing, Tom and Hania Brower and many more faculty members. I became friends with a number of students and residents whom I sometimes see including John Perri, Sam Granowitz, Peter Cohen, Herb Tauberg, Jim McMaster, Bob Greer, Kurt Niemann, Ted McClain and many more. Our "Circle of Friends" started then with Mervin and Marcia Stewart, Marshall and Lois Levy, Fred and Esther Marks and Pepper and Stephie Mallinger and I still meet almost yearly now (alas, without Marshall, Stephanie and Esther who are deceased). My family still lived in Pittsburgh so we saw Mary and Hymie occasionally and Milton and Cecille communicated with us as well. Some of the family kept track of us... Aunts Rosie, Nellie, Esther, and their families including cousins Tootsie, Morty, Gerald, Honey, Sandy, Stan Skirboll and even Sandy Green and his sister Lucille Most of the time they wanted some free medical advice, but it was still nice hear from them once in a while. Milt was still running Specialty Clothing Company but he and Cecille were going through rough times.

After my first year was up, Ferg decided to keep me. He raised my salary, gave me access to one of the secretaries in the office (not Mary, she belonged to him), increased my rank at the University to Assistant Professor and things began to look pretty good. In 1962, I became a member of the Orthopaedic Research Society and in 1964 of the American Academy of Orthopaedic Surgeons. My lab work was coming along, and by 1966, I had 24 articles in print in the Orthopaedic literature. I began traveling to meetings to give talks to orthopaedists and rheumatologists.

Mark Drive life was pretty good. We had two cars, several baby sitters (including a wonderful woman named Rachel who taught the kids how to go up and down stairs) and Carole and I and the kids spent some good summer times on Cape Cod with her parents and

133

their friends. We also got a great cat named Lydia, to whom I was allergic! Fortunately our lab person adopted her and she lived a very long time. With three children and Susie however, Carole and I decided that the house on Mark Drive was too small and the kid's school was not so great and that we ought to move to Squirrel Hill.

In 1963 we bought a house on Northumberland Street, which by standards of all the other places we had lived over time, was a mansion!

The house at 5544 Northumberland Street was very special. It had a small front porch, a nice driveway and a two-car garage. The back yard was big and very green in the summer time and a nice place to sit. The house had a very large living room, a beautiful dining room, a good kitchen and a dinette. On the second floor there were three bedrooms and two baths and a den where I could keep my books and journals. We bought our first color television set and put it into one of the little dens on the second floor and that was exciting. It was much easier to get to work and indeed Forbes Street and Murray Avenue were within walking distance. We even became interested in becoming members of a Synagogue on Forbes Street about two blocks away from our home. The Manor and Beacon movie theaters were a few blocks away and the Squirrel Hill Theater, Poli's restaurant and the Hot Puppy Shop were close by as well. Other good places to eat included the Hebrew National Delicatessen, a great steak house on Forbes Street and a good fish restaurant not far from the Beacon Theater. It was easy for Carole to shop for food or for other necessities for the children or the house. We reconnected with our friends in Squirrel Hill at this point and since Mervin moved to Beacon Street and Stephanie and Pepper and Marshall and Lois all lived north of Forbes, we once again started the Circle of Friends. Even Lennie and Millie Schwartz lived close to us on Northumberland Street but they were never very friendly. The kids started at Whitman School, a much better place than in Verona.

In 1965, I became an Associate Professor at Pitt and in 1966, I received an invitation to consider the opportunity to become Chief of Orthpaedics at the Hospital for Joint Diseases and Professor and Co-Chairman at Mount Sinai Hospital and Medical School. My favorite colleague Tom Brower had moved to Tennessee and we now had Bob Greer and Kurt Niemann as our new junior faculty members. I talked to Ferg and asked him what he thought about that offer and what his advice was. He replied that he didn't think I could do much more at Pitt and he thought I really ought to take the job. So I did and we all moved back to New York.

Back to New York City and the Hospital for Joint Diseases

We moved in 1966 and it was not exactly a happy time for the kids who by that time were pretty much into life in Squirrel Hill. Allison was 10, David was 8 and Keith was 5. Susie was getting old and was beginning to slow down. I was 38 and Carole was 35 and it was a really big move. We bought a house in Scarsdale, not terribly far away from the north end of Harlem and it was a very nice place. It was located at 50 Brewster Road, on the corner of Butler and just like the street names, it was a pretty sophisticated neighborhood. The school system was great and Allison and David had a great time and they both made a lot of very good friends, some of whom they are still in contact with. Keith started in Fox Meadow School across from our house a year after we

135

got there and when we moved out five years afterwards, he was just beginning junior high.

The house itself was spectacular. We had a beautiful living room, a big dining area two steps down, a very large kitchen and a back porch overlooking a big yard that I loved. Upstairs were our bedrooms and a sort of a den half a floor up. We had a special room just above the staircase which was where our family turtle, Jimmella lived, who I think would have lived forever if we hadn't given her away when we moved to Boston in 1972. We also had two famous guinea pigs, Piggy and Max. We also found a baby robin, whom we named Morris Robin and despite my attempts I was never able to teach him to fly. During our stay in Scarsdale, poor old Susie developed a malignant melanoma and metastases and in 1970, we had to put her away…a brutally sad day for all of us. Fortunately we were able to get another Susie, who looked just like the first cocker spaniel, who we kept paper trained for all her life. She moved to Boston with us in 1972.

I was the chief at HJD beginning 1966 and although I had limited status at Mt. Sinai, I got to know and enjoy working with Bob Siffert at that facility. He and Miriam were friendly and involved us in a number of social activities at their hospital. Other friends included two of the staff from my residency days, Alex Norman and Al Betcher and they and their wives helped us find our way in the Hospital and with the new staff. Howard Dorfman was another friend in the Pathology world along with Golden Selin.

Although I was respected and in many ways strongly supported, I believe the Orthopaedic Staff had mixed emotions about me. I was young by their standards and some of the older members considered me still a resident! I developed a laboratory with a group of scientists and they weren't sure what the work on cartilage meant to them or to the world of orthopaedics. Despite the concern of the faculty as to my research activities, I became President of the Orthopaedic Research Society in 1969 and had a really busy crew who did some very good research and were well funded by the NIH. I remained close to my teachers, Joe Milgram, Joe Buchman, Mannie Kaplan, Charlie Sutro, Mike Burman and the rest, but they weren't really sure that I should be the chief. I devoted myself to improving the quality of care in a number of areas such as hand surgery, (by appointing Richard Smith and Bob Leffert), pediatric surgery, (by doing it myself since Leo and Barney had reduced their activities), and later I added Charlie Weiss and Michael Ehrlich to the teams as well as key players in other disciplines. I really worked hard at residency education, starting my infamous breakfast conferences, grand rounds on Saturdays, resident thesis days for their presentations, and anatomy sessions. I really think that the resident education was my best accomplishment and certainly the residents that I trained in those 6 years still comment on this. I also did my first allograft (bone transplant from another human) in November of 1971 on a very nice 16 year-old girl from upstate New York, using a distal femur from a 17 year-old girl who had died that morning at Montefiore Hospital (the graft lasted until 1996...25 years!). Years later, the former residents and I held a reunion which was lots of fun. It was also very gratifying when I returned to HJD to give the Robert Jones Lecture in 2001, to see that they all turned out to greet me. I wrote obituaries for some of the greats including Manny Kaplan, Joe Milgram and Henry Jaffe but I don't really think that the Institution views me very positively particularly since I left in 1972, only 6 years after I got there, to go to the Massachusetts General Hospital and Harvard, despite their lofty plans to expand and move to another site. Part of the problem was that they decided to go to 18th Street instead of to the campus of Mt. Sinai, where Bob Siffert and I thought we could make a really great academic impact. Anyway, when the Dean of Harvard Medical School appeared in my office in October of 1971, Carole and I decided to go to Boston and in March of 1972, I left Carole and the kids in Scarsdale with the guinea pig Max and our new sweet Susie. They joined me in June after the kids got out of school, but alas, neither the turtle nor the robin came along…neither survived our departure. Speaking of not surviving, my brother Milton died in 1970 at the age of 54; my father died in 1971 at the age of 82 and our sweet first dog Susie died in the same year at 17…a really bad time for Carole, the kids and especially me.

Early days in Boston, Harvard and the MGH (1972-1980)

They gave me a farewell party at HJD in February and in March, I drove to Boston, leaving the family in Scarsdale while the kids finished the school year. I moved in with Ann and Harold at 1691 Commonwealth Avenue and they took very good care of me. I succeeded Melvin Glimcher who had been Chief of Orthopaedics at the MGH for two years and was not really considered a great contributor. He had a decent lab on the 10th floor (now the 11th due to some clever floor renumbering recently) of the Jackson Building but he took everything away (even the clocks on the walls!) and when Antra Zarins, Lou Lippiello and I moved in we had to start from scratch. I didn't go to Boston alone. I took four Jewish boys with me, namely Dick Smith, Bob Leffert, Charlie

Weiss and Michael Ehrlich, a shock to the very Gentile Harvard orthodoxy. We all moved in over the next few months, and the hospital gave us office space on the 6th floor of the Gray Building next to the Smith Petersen Orthopaedic Library. We weren't really sure what we should try to do with the Orthopaedic Service, since a lot of the staff had moved out when Glimcher took over, but many of them came back which strengthened our position. Richard Smith was a hand surgeon and took that service over; Bob Leffert decided to be a shoulder and rehabilitation person and took over the rehab floor of White 9; Charlie Weiss decided that trauma might be good for him; and Michael became a superb pediatric orthopaedist. I wasn't sure what I should do but it seemed to me that there were no orthopaedic oncologists in Boston, so that's what I became. I also became a bone bank person based on my experience with using bone transplants (allografts) and started a very reputable bone bank in cooperation with the Boston Organ Bank Group. With the later help of Bill Tomford and Sam Doppelt, we developed the standard at the time and became major contributors to the American Association of Tissue Banks.

I had some difficulty with a few of the staff members who felt that my attention to academics and more specifically teaching and research interfered with their private practice and that bringing in four additional full time physicians really interfered with their lifestyles. I overcame their resistance but it wasn't always easy and I think there are still some people who really would be have been happy if I hadn't joined the staff. My lab people were wonderful. Antra Zarins, Lou Lippiello and later Ben Treadwell, Carol Trahan, Chris Towle and all the rest were dedicated and really productive. Between 1972 and 1980 we published 78 papers mostly in peer-reviewed journals and a lot about articular cartilage, cartilage healing and osteoarthritis. We had NIH money for several of these projects and in 1975, I received the Kappa Delta Award for Outstanding Orthopaedic Research from the American Academy of Orthopaedic Surgery. In 1977, I also received the Shands Award from the American Orthopaedic Association for my team's collective research efforts.

Shortly after I arrived I started the dreaded breakfast conferences with the residents and worked very hard to introduce science, pathophysiology and history into their discipline and I think that may have been my most successful educational activity. I had to good fortune to be able to work closely with greats such as John Hall at Boston Children's Hospital, Gus White at the Beth Israel and especially Clement Sledge at what would become Brigham and Women's, in running the residency and it became without much doubt the best residency in Orthopaedics in the country. We all worked hard and it showed!

I developed some good friends at the MGH who supported me and helped me accomplish the things I thought were important. Ed Wyman, Carter Rowe, Bert Zarins (Antra's brother!), Dinesh Patel, Hugh Chandler, Arthur Boland were very supportive (much more so than William Harris or Bob Boyd or some of the others). I brought in some senior people who were very helpful. These included Crawford Campbell, LeRoy Lavine and Paul Curtiss, who along with their wives became close friends to Carole and me.

On a more personal note, Carole, the kids and the new Susie moved to Brookline, a town surrounded by Boston, and we found a house: a 100 year old "mansion" at the corner of Dean Road and Chestnut Hill Avenue, which we bought for less than $100,000! It proved to be a fine place for us in terms of ease of transport to the Hospital, proximity to Harold and Ann, ease for shopping and social activities and just a great and safe neighborhood. Allison had just finished her junior year at Scarsdale High School and would have been devastated if she had to enter another high school in Boston. Her remarkable scholastic achievements helped get her admitted to Massachusetts Institute of Technology and subsequently to Princeton. David and Keith were accepted as students at Buckingham Browne and Nichols School and thrived, both going on to Harvard for college. Our new Susie stayed paper trained and loved her new home.

The house itself was great. We had a team of carpenters and house builders, etc. come in and made over some of the more decrepit areas and eventually we ended with a beautiful living room, a library with lots of books and a place to play music; a kitchen, a beautiful dining room that we rarely use, a breakfast room where we always ate, and a den for Henry with a place for his enormous collection of books and journals, computers, etc. On the second floor were bedrooms for Henry and Carole, for Allison, for David and for Keith, with two bathrooms and two alcoves for storage of items. We also have an enormous third floor that is a storage place for all kinds of things and a basement which included a dark room for David's photography and lots and lots of storage space which we later used for stuff that Harold and Annie left us on their passing. There are also vast collections of slides and pathologic material willed to me by the esteemed pathologists Crawford Campbell and Henry Jaffe. We filled the house with great furniture, rugs, desks and bookcases for everyone and some really great chandeliers. It really became a "mansion" and we have been very happy there from the time of our move!

So what did we do for fun in Boston? Well just about everything. We went to movies: the Circle Theatre was a block away, Chestnut Hill Theatre was in the shopping mall, the Coolidge was at Coolidge Corner just down the street, the Dedham was easy to get to and the Nicolodeon was a great place near Boston University (all of these but the Coolidge are now gone!). We had always loved movies and devoured everything that opened as well as the great classic film revivals. At some point we connected with the American Repertory Theater at Harvard and saw three or four good theatre productions there every year. We went out to dinner in lots of places. We started going to the North End for Italian food but our favorite restaurants there always seemed to burn down. We switched to places closer to home for Mexican at the Sol Azteca on Beacon Street, Italian at Bertucci's or Papparazzi's and a favorite for Chinese food at the Golden Temple on Beacon Street. We had good Jewish food at Rubins on Harvard Street and wonderful fish dinners at Legal Sea Food.

Carole and I had some great friends from the very first days we arrived in Boston. LeRoy and Dorothy Lavine were special (we had known them more casually in New York) and we went to theatre with them and dined out frequently. We saw the Campbells periodically and also Paul and Maria Curtiss. We were friendly with the Lefferts, the Ehrlichs and the Weiss's and did lots of social things with other staff members. Our best friends however were Sonny and Paul Rogal, Carole and my matchmakers, and we did everything together. We went to Tanglewood in the Western part of the state for music every summer, to Bermuda every winter and to lots of places in the city to eat or see movies or just to be together. We got to know some of their friends including Ira and Marcia Molay who we saw in Bermuda in the winter and Harry and Ruth Wechsler, who became every other month Sunday night dinner companions and occasional travel-mates. Carole and I and the kids went to the Cape with Harold and Ann in the summertime the first year we moved, just as we had done from both Pittsburgh and Scarsdale. We always had some good times there at Onset Beach on Buzzards Bay. The kids loved it as did sweet old Susie! Carole retained close friendship with her cousin Joan Wechsler and her husband, Henry and also with her cousin Ira Mogul who was then married to Margaret and living in Naples, Florida, but a constant presence on the telephone and coming up for his beloved Boston Chinese food. We occasionally saw some of her other cousins including Joan's sister Harriet, Eddie Phillips and some others from Washington or California. I, of course retained my continued relationship with Mary in Pittsburgh (who I visited several times a year including always on her birthday on Christmas Eve!), with Arthur and Shirley and their kids, Eric, Joanie, Ruthy and Daniel who by now lived far away in California, and with my sister-in-law Cecille and her children, Judy, Ricky and Bobby who at the time still lived in Pittsburgh.

We also traveled a lot for vacations in those days. We went to England with the kids several times...I took Allison and David to Hawaii once and Carole and I went there on two other occasions. We went to Italy...to Rome and especially to Florence with the kids and they loved it. In my later years when I was President of various organizations, Carole and I went to Japan, Korea, Thailand, Australia, New Zealand, England, Canada, Argentina, Scotland, South Africa, Greece, Italy,

France, Spain, Israel and Switzerland. As part of my involvement in these activities I was awarded honorary membership in the Japanese, Thai, Australian, Argentine, New Zealand, British, Canadian and Israel Orthopaedic Associations and became an Honorary Fellow of the Royal College of Surgeons of England. I was part of an extraordinary visiting program in Soviet Russia in the early '70s and was one of the first Western orthopaedists to travel to South Korea (in 1978). Those were very busy but really good days and we made lots of friends and enjoyed happy times in lots of beautiful places. We particularly loved going to Florence and to Bologna and to Venice and to parts of Japan and to New Zealand....our favorite sites for travel! When Paul became ill and Sonny developed breast cancer and sent him off to Phoenix to live, we started taking as many of the kids and grandkids to Bermuda every year from Christmas Day to New Year's Day and that became one of the great family activities. David has never been on those trips but all the rest have and we have accumulated lots of photographs and beautiful memories of days in Bermuda first, at the Newstead and more recently at Elbow Beach. One other wonderful gift to us was when Allison sent a beautiful dog, Hsaio Long back to us from Taiwan...she became a good friend of Susie 2 and an adored child of Henry and Carole for 22 wonderful years!

We also had some sad, sad memories: While living in Boston we saw family and friend's deaths that were very depressing. Aunt Sally died in 1980 at age 81 and Harold Pinkney died in 1985 at age 85. His wife Annie followed in 1990 at age 87. Mary Mankin died in 1991 at 104. Her birthday was on Christmas Eve so for the last 10 or so years of her life I went to Pittsburgh to take her out to dinner on that night. Sonny Rogal died in 1996 at age

65 and Paul died in 1997 at age 70. I gave the eulogies for both of them at their funerals in Sharon Memorial Cemetery. My sister-in-law Shirley and my brother Arthur died far away in California and recently the next generation was shocked by the death of my dear niece, Joanie, Art and Shirley's second child. Two more sad events were when sweet Susie died in 1982 at age 10 and then Hsiao Long died in 1997 at 22 years of age. And of course the loss of my sweet Carole has been impossible to get over.

The rest of good life for Henry and Carole in Boston 1980-2012

From 1980 to 2012, Carole and I watched our kids succeed in life. Allison went to Princeton, met Jim Carton, went to Taiwan, came back and married, became a computer person and established herself as a giant in the Internet. She and Jim are the parents of two wonderful, wonderful children, Sam and Molly who have filled their grandparents' hearts with joy. David went to Harvard and then to University of Virginia and got his PhD in Classics, took a great job and tenure at Cornell. David lives a good life in his own house with his cats but alas still smokes and drinks lots of beer. Keith graduated from Harvard, was a singer with considerable talent, went to Pitt Medical School, met Julia and married her. He took his residency in Orthopaedics at Harvard (with me as his chairman!) and she became a radiologist and they did well at the MGH and BWH for a while until they decided to move in 2000 to get away from the bad things that were happening at our hospital. They moved to North Carolina and then on to Dallas, TX. They have a wonderful son, Cameron who can do everything wonderfully well.

145

Carole became a great research librarian. She got her Masters in Library Science from Simmons College and became an accomplished and published force in her field. She worked at the Treadwell Library at the MGH for over 30 years and became a very important figure in the Friends of the Cancer Center and was a great asset to their grant program. I had the delight of working with her on a program called "Dialogues" along with our good friend Trudi Fondren in which we allowed our audience of cancer patients and their families to hear and discuss aspects of their problems with experts in the field. It ran for about 16 years and was very well received.

Carole was a superb mother and grandmother and of course the love of my life. In 2011, she was diagnosed with a brain cancer and just a few weeks after our sixtieth anniversary, she went off to become an angel in heaven. I miss her every day.

In 1995, Harvard decided to make radical changes to a number of their hospitals and part of the effort was to replace me as chief of Orthopaedics. I stopped doing surgery and after a few years left clinical practice altogether. Since the turn of the century I have had heart surgery, prostate surgery and a few major sicknesses. I am stiff and sore most of the time, but I still make it into the lab and my office four days a week. I mostly read e-mails but I still write a little and I still get the chance to teach whenever anybody agrees to listen to me. I continued to teach my bone physiology course at the Academy until a few years ago and I have many talks which I can give at the drop of a hat, although most of my lectures now are close to home. I still get to Pittsburgh around two times a year and meet with our ever dwindling circle of friends. I have slowed done but, as I tell everyone who asks, I'm "holding it together."

A professional life

The final note in this section is related to me, and my time as an orthopaedic surgeon. I worked very hard for a long time and did I think a lot of good things. I performed over 20,000 surgeries in a career lasting over 40 years. I can't even think of how many patients I saw in the clinic. I used to joke that every single one of my surgical patients called me every day to complain, even the ones who had died!

My clinical contributions include the establishment of bone banking standards for transplant, the development of safe techniques for limb salvage in orthopaedic cancers, progress in the treatment of many types of cancers and a history of well cared for patients. I still receive cards and letters from patients I can barely remember telling me that I saved their lives and that makes me proud and happy for all my work.

My research labs helped define the protein composition of cartilage as well as parts of the cascade that lead to cartilage destruction in arthritis and other disease states. I helped pioneer the use of Flow Cytometry to evaluate the cellularity of types of bone cancers as well as to predict their response to therapeutic agents. I was proud to have continued funding by the national Institute of health and other prestigious organizations for more than forty years and I still have a grant (working with my old lab mate Carol Trahan) for the digitization of the pathology collections that were bequeathed to me and which live in the basement at Dean Road. In my last years of clinical practice, I developed a computerized system for recording data for our tumor service that I still hope will become a standard in the field, and it now has searchable information for 18,000 patients with bone and soft tissue tumors. So my scientific contribution continues (I hope!).

In teaching, I trained forty years' worth of resident physicians in Pittsburgh, New York and Boston and taught over 100 clinical and research fellows from all over the world in our Orthopaedic Oncology Fellowship program. I taught musculoskeletal science to generations of medical students, most of whom probably didn't care that much for the lessons. I served as President of the Orthopaedic Research Society, the Academic Orthopaedic Society, the American Orthopaedic Association, the American Board of Orthopaedic Surgery and the Musculoskeletal Tumor Society and was on numerous committees for other organizations. I have served on the Dean's Visiting Committee for the University of Pittsburgh for 13 years, have a chair in my name at that Institution, received an award as a Distinguished Alumnus and as Legacy Laureate from them. In 1990 I received the Bristol-Meyers-Squibb-Zimmer Award for Distinguished Achievement in Orthopaedic Research. Currently I have almost 650 articles in print, mostly in refereed journals and I gave the Instructional Courses in Cartilage and in Metabolic Bone Diseases as well as other topics at the American Academy of Orthopaedic Surgery Meetings for 27 continuous years.

I have always said that in the Jewish faith a man's immortality is based on the memory that he leaves behind. I have two sons and a daughter and three grandchildren to carry on my name and my legacy. I have thousands of surrogate sons and daughters in the students that I have always taught. There are tens of thousands (or more) patients whose lives I touched ...I hope for the better! I don't want to live forever, especially not that my sweet Carole is gone. But with all these people talking about me, who knows ...I just may!

CHAPTER 6: PROLOGUE: LIFE WITH HENRY AND CAROLE – by KEITH MANKIN

Most of the memories in the chapters above were written in the mid to late 1990's and have been revised to keep up with all the changes that time brings. My dad couldn't track down all the lives and deaths of the many, many characters that he mentioned, but he has noted the sad passage of time with each passing friend and family member.

My mother's death two years ago shook him to the core. As you read his memories you see what a constant she was for him from the very first fateful meeting in 1951. In each other's eyes they are always young and carefree and the spirit of their love continues to whisper to him.

Henry's presence dominated the nuclear family. Our schedules, our vacations, where we lived were all based on the needs of his professional life. But unlike some overachievers, we never felt he was a stranger in the household. The house reflected my mother's elegant and traditional taste, but the walls rang with his larger than life humor, his music and his personality. Meals were loud and exuberant events, often involving quizzes and other interactive conversations to include the whole family, even the dogs. Our trips together, often crammed into his ridiculously small sports cars, were whirlwinds of walking through cities and viewing art in all its forms, trying to fit as much of a location into the time we had as possible. Henry and Carole took us to movies (often Avant garde and foreign!), theater, opera, ballet and museums, not so much to provide us with culture (although that was the result) but because that was how they wanted to fill their lives. Is it any wonder that my sister, brother and I can only blink at the speed of our childhoods?

Henry slows down for only a few things. He loved the time with his pets. As he discussed in the last chapter, dogs, cats (to which he was severely allergic), preternaturally long-lived turtles and even rescued robins all were enveloped by his love. He would come home from work and time would stop while he would cuddle either of the Susies or Hsiao Long. Until my mother's death, it seemed that his deepest grieving was for the passing of the animals in his life.

He also slowed down, at least in his early years, for his art and music. An accomplished oboist in high school, he continued to play the recorder for years and my Sunday memories are sweetened by the image of him and Carole playing duets (Mom was capable at the piano and loved to sing). For years in Pittsburgh, New York and our annual summer pilgrimages to Cape Cod, he would dabble in watercolor painting. He developed a broad primitive style which could capture space and motion well and fit into a 1960's sensibility. His Pittsburgh series captures the earthy gloom and homeliness of the city on the eve of its fall and rise. His Cape Cod paintings are full of warmth and peace. But I think his New York paintings are the best of his works. His images of Spanish Harlem and particular a bird's eye view of the Apollo Theater are redolent of jazz and grit, a city with attitude but not yet danger or despair.

I could write an entire book about Carole, and in fact may just do so. She was innately more shy than my father, but if she knew you (or if you crossed her) you always knew exactly what she was thinking. She was a Renaissance woman, even from her early childhood – drawing, writing and reading. Her love of books lasted for her entire life and the houses where we lived were crowded with friendly stacks of the beloved works. She loved music and culture and was successful in nudging Henry away from his work to a wide array of events (even if she was not always successful at keeping him awake).

She graduated from Boston University with a degree in psychology and a keen curiosity about life. I always felt she would have been a wonderful primary care doctor. She was intuitive, empathetic, compassionate but also not afraid to push people for their own good.

She was also the glue that held the family together. Not only was she there always to take care of us, she made sure that we stayed in contact with our father, no matter how busy he was. Even if that meant being pulled out of bed to see him while he ate a sandwich coming home late. She also helped him entertain staff and colleagues and visiting dignitaries.

As we grew up and my father did less entertaining at home, Carole focused on her own professional life, obtaining an advanced degree and a career as a research librarian at her beloved Treadwell library. She was spared seeing the dissolution of the last of the great private academic libraries when Treadwell closed its doors forever in 2013. I still think I felt earth tremors coming from Sharon Memorial Park at that time.

In his work and professional life Henry was indefatigable. He dominated and took the orthopaedic world by the throat, sometimes quite literally. He was a chairman first at 38 years of age, a time when most surgeons are just beginning to establish themselves in their specialties. He was the Chief of Orthopaedics at the Massachusetts General Hospital (and de facto chair of the Harvard Orthopaedic Program) at the ridiculously young age of 44. As he alluded to, there was some resentment at his meteoric rise, but he carried his programs upwards with him. Hospital for Joint Diseases is one of the most prestigious orthopaedic facilities in the country and the MGH and Harvard Orthopaedics still maintains the excellence that he achieved. Almost a hundred of his former residents and fellows have gone on to chairman positions at other programs and continue to teach his words and his lessons.

The effect of Henry Mankin on orthopaedics and the medical world can be measured in global terms. When he first burst onto the scene, orthopaedists had a fairly crude reputation. To be sure there were great minds in the field, but most of the bone doctors of the day were looked on as strong and plodding, like draught horses. There is an old joke that the way to choose the orthopaedic class was to hit medical students on the head with a sledge hammer and the ones still standing would be orthopods. There is another which states that orthopaedists are strong as oxen and almost twice as smart. As an orthopaedist myself, I find these jokes dismissive and harsh, but the reputation was unquestionably there.

Henry Mankin came along and attracted the attention of the scientific world (not just the clinical one) with his research accomplishments. He obtained the first ever NIH grant for an orthopaedist and had an unprecedented 45 years of continuous government funding not for clinical studies, or the mechanical research that was the usual sphere of the bone doctors, but in the rigorous studies of biochemistry and physiology. HJM was a man who could discuss and dispute with both the surgeons and the scientists all in the course of a day's work. His example gave birth to other thinkers and others researchers in the field. Suddenly orthopaedics became known for its intellectual rigor. There was still room for the former football players, but they had better be top of their class to get there. The sledge hammer would not favor them anymore.

The global reach is seen in the positions he has held in every major international orthopaedic society. He traveled to every continent (save Antarctica) and his name and repute reached every orthopaedist in the world. Two years ago, when I traveled to Seoul, South Korea to speak about pediatric spine there was more buzz about the man who had retired almost 15 years

153

before than there was about me or any of the active participants at the conference.

In 1995, he received the unprecedented honor of election to the Royal College of Surgeons in Great Britain. It was almost unheard of for any American to receive that honor, let alone, gasp, an American orthopaedist.

Henry earned his reputation not only on the basis of his legendary intellectual accomplishments but also on his often heroic patient care. He has always been a man who has let his curiosity and passion guide his endeavors. As a result, he reinvented himself at almost every major juncture in his career. He started out, as he told us, interested in internal medicine (in fact gastroenterology, which he agrees would have been a miserable field to pursue). When the Navy provided him with an abundance of bones and joints to work on, he became passionately interested in musculoskeletal medicine, although he might well have gone into Obstetrics for all the babies that he delivered in that impressionable time. He arrived in Pittsburgh for his first staff job, where his mentor gives him the one open position, pediatric orthopaedics, and he becomes a giant in the field. Several of his early papers in that subspecialty are still considered classics. He moved on to Joint Diseases where his interest in cartilage metabolism led him to be an arthritis specialist. Finally, at the MGH, he saw an underserved area which captivated his long-held fascination with pathology and he became perhaps the finest orthopaedic oncologist that the world has ever known.

At each stop, his intense approach to patient care and his legendary work ethic guided him and influenced those around him. How could a junior staff physician think about leaving early or not coming in on a Saturday when he or she knew that the Chairman will be there, working with an energy that put far younger men to shame.   There were many times during my residency and the years I served on staff when I wished I had a less energetic role model.   But he was not just about hard work and strenuous effort.   One of the things that we all learned at his side was that healing welled up from belief and emotion.   The most skilled hands would not heal a patient if they weren't backed with a firm resolve to cure.   Henry Mankin could make a deep and lasting connection with a patient in the briefest of interactions because for that amount of time the patient sensed that she was the most important thing in Henry's life.

I shared many patients with my father and heard the stories of many more.   I helped him fix the hip of one of his childhood romances and save the life of a young man who had been dismissed as having a groin pull when he actually had a pelvic cancer.   For many years, I tried to get him to write down some of the stories, to capture the immense humanity of the work that he had done, but he has always demurred.   In our modern age of Health Privacy, most of the stories can be told in only the most abstract of terms, but Henry is a product of the pre-HIPAA days when a doctor could paste his office walls with pictures of his fine results if he so chose.   My father never shied from boasting about his procedures or his research, but he always held off on boasting about his patient   interactions.   It   was,   perhaps,   that   his relationship   with   the   patient   was   too   intense   and personal to make public.

I'll repeat just a small sampling of the wonders that Henry achieved.   One case was that of a young lady who had a bad tumor in her pelvis.   My father performed a life and limb saving procedure which resulted in the removal of part of her pelvic bone.   She presented later with what appeared to be a recurrent mass.   The MRI showed that the mass was not a cancer; it was a baby girl.   Careful planning and preparation allowed the child to be brought to term and delivered in good health.   A picture hanging on my parents' kitchen wall shows my father recently beaming with pride at her Bat Mitzvah; his miracle baby.

Another patient had a leg tumor that required removal when she was in her teens. I recall her coming out to dinner with my parents, my Harvard-matriculating brother and his college roommate. She was in awe of those two mature and polished gentlemen. I was in awe of her poise and her spirit, despite the catastrophic deal that life had given her. Not long ago, when I lived in North Carolina, I was contacted by her. She had seen my name and had looked me up. We met for lunch and she regaled me with stories that I had never heard about her rehabilitation and her recovery. She had been as bratty as any youngster of her age and was determined to rebel as much as she could. But she was overwhelmed by the huge surge of affection, of compassion and of tough take-your-medicine-and-like-it, I-worked-hard-for-you-now-you-work-hard-for-me energy that my father provided her. He compelled her to get better. She went on in medicine, working as a successful physical therapist, despite having only one leg.

Some of the stories are too sad to tell. I have helped my father sort information on patients with terrible cancers that were even beyond his will-power to treat. He would recite their names like the knoll of a church bell, the dark cloud of his own human limitations weighing on his brow. I have felt honored to share in these reflective moments with him but also frustrated that there was nothing I could do to remind him how many lives he saved and how many happy years he has added to patients who were otherwise doomed.

His somber moments were few in his heyday and the overwhelming picture that people have of my father is his huge humor, replete with a booming and infectious laugh. My dad has always seen the funny side of every situation that he could, until of course my mother's death. Even then he can still find the spirit to summon forth the image of her coming to him in his dreams. "I'll be joining you in time," he says to her shade which laughs. "Like you're coming anywhere near heaven," she says. That is classic (and healthy) Henry Mankin humor.

Humor is the birthright of the mankin (and in fact the Pinkney) family. I have heard my father tell an audience of Chasidim that if there are two thing Jews know, it's how to laugh in the face of tragedy and where to find great Chinese food. His mother Mary scoffed at hardship, scraping the meat off a chicken back to get one more serving and mimicking the butcher as she did so. She maintained her wonderful and acidic humor to the very end of her life. Once, at well over a hundred years old, with Henry visiting her at the Jewish Home for the Aged she persisted in calling him Arthur. Henry, concerned that she may finally be slipping from reality gently corrected her, but she continued to call him by his brother's name. Finally, he told her, "Mary, I'm, not Arthur. I'm Henry." Mary clucked her tongue. "Nonsense," she said, "Henry could never be as old or as fat as you." With one blow she had cut two sons down to size.

Henry Mankin's humor remains broad. I have had to tell him that a neurologic check is not the best time for him to joke that his name is "Irving Schultz," but at the same examination, when the doctor asked whom the Vice-President was, Henry asked, "Would you know the Vice-President's name if it wasn't written down for you?" Touché. His humor is also physical. There are many, many pictures of him pinching cheeks and playfully choking his protégées. But it is most often to a pointed effect. One of his most famous lectures is on Calcium and Phosphorus metabolism in the body. When there is too much of both of the minerals in the bloodstream they tend to join together into an insoluble salt. Dr. Mankin would talk about the fate of Lot's wife and illustrate the effect of the unhappy reaction by freezing in his tracks as he shows how a person "turns to stone." Anyone who has ever seen the lecture will remember it forever; the gleeful growl of the speaker, the build-up in energy and the moment when he stands, statue-like, for the perfect number of comedic beats, before releasing, his point made and understood.

In an unguarded moment, Henry once told me that he wished he had a career like the late great actor Zero Mostel. There is a great deal in his persona that is reminiscent of the originator of Tevye or Max Bialystock. Both are loud. Both are unquestionably larger than life. Both will play for the great laugh. But both have a poignancy and a sweetness that makes them heartwarming, loveable and a bit frightening to behold. I think my father would have been a great musical theater performer and that the stage lost a true star when he stepped into the medical field.

It was hard to be a resident under Henry Mankin's tutelage. I like to tell people I have the scars that he gave me and more. He was demanding, he was cutting, he was ruthless – but never more with his students than he was with himself. Unlike others in the field, though, he could be amazingly empathetic. He would tell you when you had done well as sure as he would hide you for messing up. In orthopaedics, we have to sit for an oral examination after two years of practice. Generations of examinees dreaded coming in and finding the mustachioed giant as there tester. Several even threw up at his feet. But he would always try to guide them to success. He was scary because of his knowledge and his excellence, but not because of his behavior unlike other board examiners who held their evil sway.

Four mornings a week, every week for forty plus years, Henry sat down for breakfast with his resident staff. These meetings were as legendary as the great man himself.   Most often there would be unidentified x-rays which would be read by one of the house officers and then discussed by another or most often many others. The cases ran the gamut from strange tumors to congenital deformities. Sometimes, Dr. Mankin would be content to talk about the case in hand.   There were always teaching points aplenty, if only on how to read and interpret the x-rays and generate a differential diagnosis.   Sometimes, he would have no interest in what was presented on the board. He might say, "If the x-ray showed this instead, what would it be?" or "If this were an hand and not a leg, what would this be?" Generations of residents bet and lost hypothetical zlotys (a Polish currency) on the correct answer to his tortuous questions.   At other times, in the midst of a crisis, he would ignore the case and simply relate to the young doctors in his teaching fold.   Sometimes, if the mood was on him or the moon was full, he would ask questions about poetry or theater. A house officer (or "house cat" as he liked to call us) would be assigned a report and had better come back the next day with wondrous things to pronounce.

We all complained bitterly. It's not like we didn't have enough work to do without the added burden of looking up poems by William Blake ("Tyger, tyger, burning bright") or the arcane association between Professor Moriarty and Captain Nemo (which actually exists!). But when the anger had died down, we realized how lucky we were to be subjected to his close attention.   Not only could we read x-rays better than anyone, but we could prepare talks and teach with skill and aplomb. We also realized that his presence was not a punishment but an act of grace bestowed upon us, the lucky few. In the end, we loved him for it.

I see my father now, a Tyger burning not quite as bright as he nears his nineties. Like him, I always think of the fearsome and formidable man that he was in his prime with my redoubtable mother always at his side. His is a great Jewish story, a great American story, a great Orthopaedic and medical story. Above all, his is a story of families – the one that permeated Pittsburgh in the first half of the last century, the one led by my mother like royalty in Boston in the later years of the same century, and the one, extended over time and space, that looks back at his work, his teaching and his character on an almost daily basis and remembers.

34060808R00091

Made in the USA
San Bernardino, CA
17 May 2016